BedWarmers

by Lynda Milligan & Nancy Smith

POSSIBILITIES®

...Publishers of DreamSpinners® patterns, I'll Teach Myself® sewing products, and Possibilities® books...

AF207709

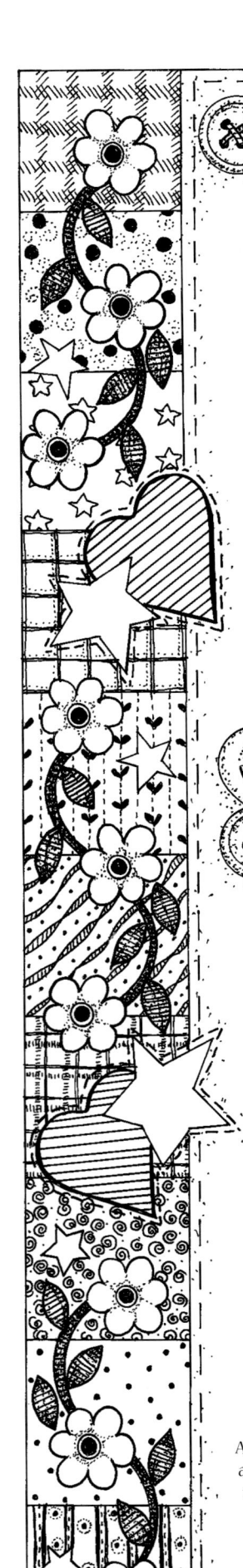

Acknowledgements

We would like to dedicate this book to our husbands, Jack Smith and Gene Milligan, who have inspired us to become the women we are today. They are loyal and flexible and continue to listen to our business challenges. They offer suggestions, fix computers, help with inventory, mop up flood water, make trips to the store in the middle of the night when our burglar alarm goes off, and just about anything else that we need. Child care is and has been a fifty-fifty proposition with all our traveling, and they continue to keep the home fires burning. They encourage us to strive for what we want from our tomorrows and support us as we venture forth to fulfill our dreams.

We thank you – we appreciate you – we love you.

Nancy & Lynda

Special Thanks

Special thanks to the following for the opportunity to photograph our quilts in their store or home:

Jan Albee
Colorado Life Styles — 9975 Wadsworth Parkway, Westminster, CO 80021
Davis and Shaw — 1434 Champa Street, Denver, CO 80202

Credits

Sharon Holmes — Editing, Technical Illustration
Debbe Linn — Cover, Photo Styling, Technical Illustration, Design
Sara Tuttle — Hand Illustration, Design
Valerie Perrone — Hand Illustration, Design
Jane Dumler — Consultation, Stitching
Joanne Malone — Consultation, Stitching
Chris Scott — Copy Reading
Brian Birlauf — Photography

Every effort has been made to ensure that the information in this book is accurate. Due to individual skills, conditions, and tools, we cannot be responsible for any losses, injuries, or other damages that may result from its use.

POSSIBILITIES®

...Publishers of DreamSpinners® patterns, I'll Teach Myself® sewing products, and Possibilities books...

BedWarmers

© 1999 Lynda Milligan & Nancy Smith

Published in the United States of America by Possibilities®, Denver, Colorado.

Library of Congress Catalog Card Number: 99-067849
ISBN: 1-880972-40-9

Photo Index

ENLARGING PATTERNS We try to fill our books with as many projects as possible. Because of this, some patterns may have to be enlarged on a copier or with a home computer/scanner setup. We know this may be an inconvenience, but we are sure you will be delighted with your finished project.

APPLIQUE Our favorite method of applique is the fusible web technique with a buttonhole stitch finish. Patterns are reversed and ready to be traced. Be sure to have plenty of fusible web on hand if using this method. Add seam allowance to patterns if doing hand applique.

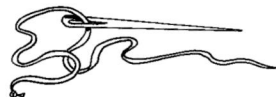 # Traditional Comforter Cover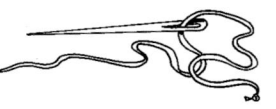

Photos on page 25.

This basic comforter cover has offset seaming on front and back and a snap tape closing at the bottom. Yardage for front and back are listed separately so different fabrics can be chosen for a reversible comforter cover.

COMFORTER SIZING Comforters come in more sizes than other bedding, so we checked many stores and catalogs before deciding on dimensions to use for our directions.

By far the most common comforter length was 86", so we settled easily on that. The variations were most commonly 90", 92", and 96". If your comforter is one of those lengths, you can add 4", 6", or 10" to the lengths in our charts. When making a longer comforter cover of any bed size, add to the given yardage (for each panel).

The widths of comforters also vary. We chose one of the more common widths in each bed size. The yardage given allows for adjustments. Simply trim fabric in Step 1e to your comforter's width.

	Twin	Double/Queen	King
Purchased Comforter Width by length	64 x 86"	86 x 86"	102 x 86"
Yardage Use 42-44"-wide fabric. Allow extra if matching plaids.			
Front	5⅜ yds.	8 yds.	8 yds.
Back	5⅜ yds.	8 yds.	8 yds.
Snap tape approx. 1" wide	62"	84"	100"

Twin

Use ½" seam allowance.

1. FRONT

   a. Cut two pieces the width of the fabric by 91".

   b. Remove selvages.

   c. Cut one piece in half lengthwise. Stitch one to each side of the remaining piece as shown.

   d. Press seams open then zigzag stitch each raw edge separately.

   e. Trim an equal amount from each side to make the cover front 65" wide.

2. BACK

   Repeat Step 1 with fabric for back.

3. ASSEMBLE

   a. Place front and back right sides together and stitch top and side edges. Trim corners. Zigzag stitch seam allowances.

   b. Hem: Press 2" to wrong side at bottom edge, then press 2" to wrong side again. Stitch close to fold. Press.

   c. Stitch snap tape to each side of bottom opening, centered on hem.

1c. Cut One Piece in Half | Stitch Each Half to Remaining Piece

1e. Trim | Trim to 65" Wide | Trim | 65" Wide x 91" Long

3a. Stitch Top & Sides

3b. Hem Bottom

3c. Stitch Snap Tape to Hem

Double/Queen

Use ½″ seam allowance.

1. FRONT

   a. Cut three pieces the width of the fabric by 91″.

   b. Remove selvages.

   c. Stitch the three pieces of fabric together as shown.

   d. Press seams open then zigzag stitch each raw edge separately.

   e. Trim an equal amount from each side to make the cover front 87″ wide.

2. BACK

   Repeat Step 1 with fabric for back.

3. ASSEMBLE

   See Step 3, page 4.

1c.

Stitch

1e.

Trim | Trim to 87″ Wide | Trim

1e.

87″ Wide
X
91″ Long

King

Use ½″ seam allowance.

1. FRONT

   a. Cut three pieces the width of the fabric by 91″.

   b. Remove selvages.

   c. Stitch the three pieces of fabric together as shown.

   d. Press seams open then zigzag stitch each raw edge separately.

   e. Trim an equal amount from each side to make the cover front 103″ wide.

2. BACK

   Repeat Step 1 with fabric for back.

3. ASSEMBLE

   See Step 3, page 4.

1c.

Stitch

1e.

Trim | Trim to 103″ Wide | Trim

1e.

103″ Wide
X
91″ Long

Overlap Comforter Cover

Photos on pages 21 and 57.

This comforter cover with a top overlap has offset seaming on front and back. Yardage amounts for the front and front overlap are listed together as well as separately so they can be made with the same fabric or with contrasting fabrics.

COMFORTER SIZING Comforters come in more sizes than other bedding, so we checked many stores and catalogs before deciding on dimensions to use for our directions.

By far the most common comforter length was 86", so we settled easily on that. The variations were most commonly 90", 92", and 96". If your comforter is one of those lengths, you can add 4", 6", or 10" to the lengths in our charts. When making a longer comforter cover of any bed size, add to the given yardage (for each panel).

The widths of comforters also vary. We chose one of the more common widths in each bed size. The yardage given allows for adjustments. Simply trim fabric in Step 1e to your comforter's width.

	Twin	Double/Queen	King
Purchased Comforter Width by length	64 x 86"	86 x 86"	102 x 86"

Yardage Use 42-44"-wide fabric. Allow extra if matching plaids. Yardage amounts for the front and front overlap are listed together as well as separately so they can be made with the same fabric or with contrasting fabrics.

	Twin	Double/Queen	King
Front & Front Overlap of Same Fabric	6⅞ yds.	10¼ yds.	10¼ yds.
Contrasting Front	5¼ yds.	7¾ yds.	7¾ yds.
Contrasting Front Overlap	1⅞ yds.	3 yds.	3 yds.
Back	5⅛ yds.	7½ yds.	7½ yds.
Binding	1⅛ yds.	1¼ yds.	1⅜ yds.
Snap tape approx. 1" wide	48"	60"	86"

Cover with Front and Front Overlap of Same Fabric

Twin

Use ½" seam allowance.

1. FRONT

   a. Cut two pieces the width of the fabric by 119".

   b. Remove selvages.

   c. Cut one piece in half lengthwise. Stitch one to each side of the remaining piece as shown.

   d. Press seams open then zigzag stitch each raw edge separately.

   e. Trim an equal amount from each side to make the cover front 65" wide.

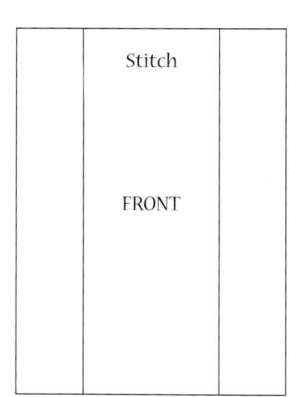

1c. Cut One Piece in Half / Stitch / FRONT

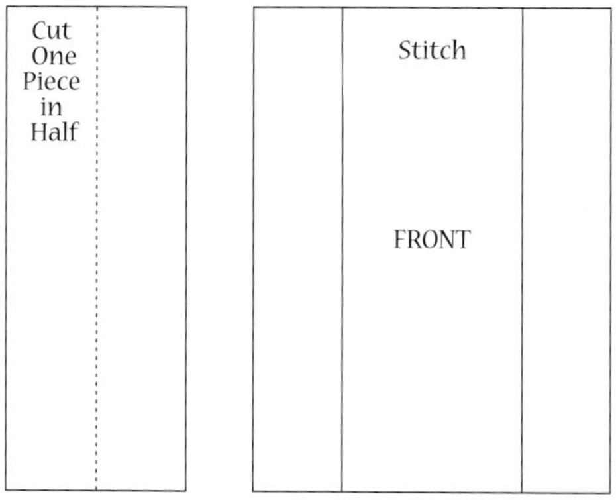

1e. Trim / Trim to 65"Wide / Trim / FRONT — 65" Wide x 119" Long / FRONT

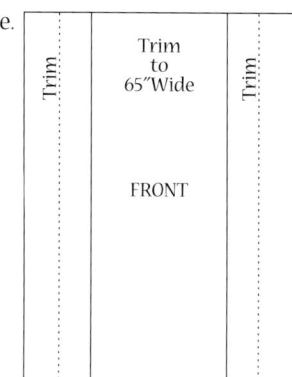
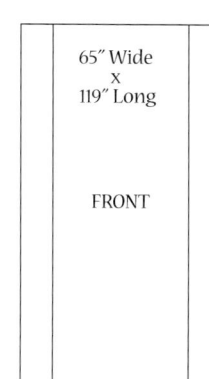

2. BACK

    a. Cut two pieces the width of the fabric by 87″.

    b. Repeat Steps 1b-e of twin directions, page 6.

3. ASSEMBLE

    a. Cut **front** into two pieces 29″ from top edge. Hem lower edge of front overlap: Press 2″ to wrong side, then press 2″ to wrong side again. Stitch close to fold. Press. Hem top edge of front in same way. Press.

    b. Pin front to back, **wrong** sides together, even at lower edge. Stitch sides and bottom.

    c. Stitch one side of snap tape to inside of front at top, close to edge, centered from side to side. Pin other side of snap tape to back, lining up snaps. Stitch in place.

    d. Pin front overlap to comforter cover, right side up, with top edges even. Stitch sides and top.

    e. Binding: Cut crossgrain strips 3¾″ wide (twin–8 strips, double/queen–9 strips, king–10 strips). Stitch all strips end to end. Press in half lengthwise, wrong sides together. Bind entire outside edge using ⅝″ seam allowance for a wide finish.

    f. Optional: Stitch buttons to front overlap for decoration.

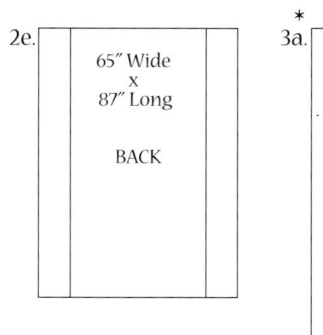

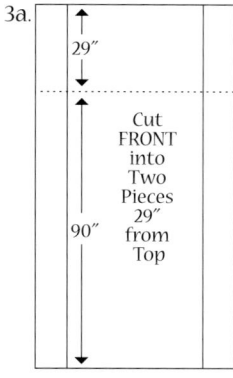

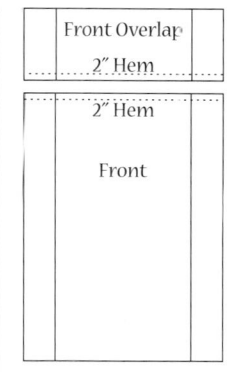

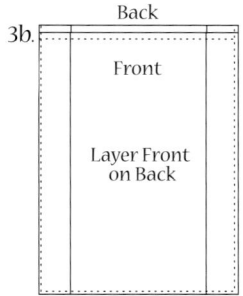

Double/Queen

Use ½″ seam allowance.

1. FRONT

    a. Cut three pieces the width of the fabric by 119″.

    b. Remove selvages.

    c. Stitch the three pieces of fabric together as shown.

    d. Press seams open then zigzag stitch each raw edge separately.

    e. Trim an equal amount from each side to make the cover front 87″ wide.

2. BACK

    a. Cut three pieces the width of the fabric by 87″.

    b. Repeat Steps 1b-e of double/queen directions, directly above.

3. ASSEMBLE

Follow Step 3a-f of twin directions at top of page.

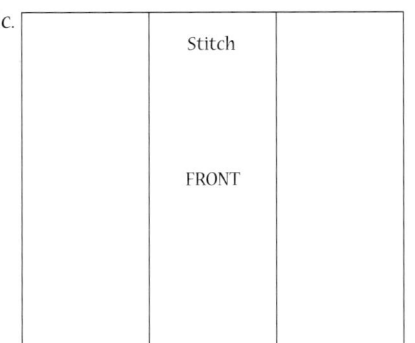

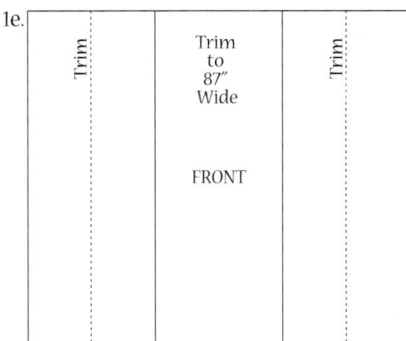

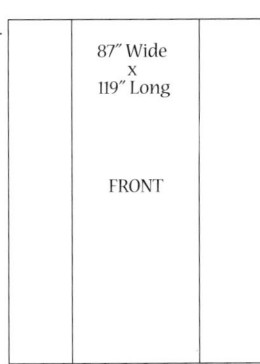

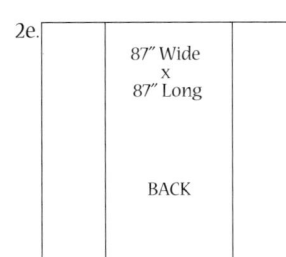

7

King

Use ½" seam allowance.

1. FRONT

   a. Cut three pieces the width of the fabric by 119".

   b. Remove selvages.

   c. Stitch the three pieces of fabric together as shown.

   d. Press seams open then zigzag stitch each raw edge separately.

   e. Trim an equal amount from each side to make the cover front 103" wide.

2. BACK

   a. Cut three pieces the width of the fabric by 87".

   b. Repeat Steps 1b-e of king directions, directly above.

3. ASSEMBLE

   Follow Step 3a-f of twin directions, page 7.

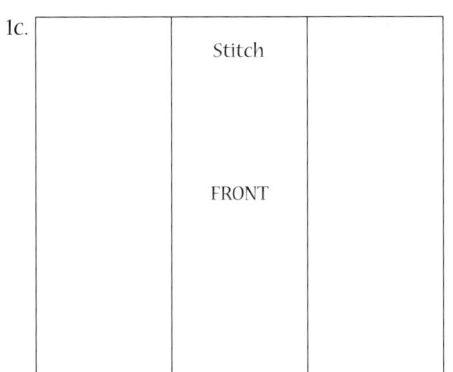

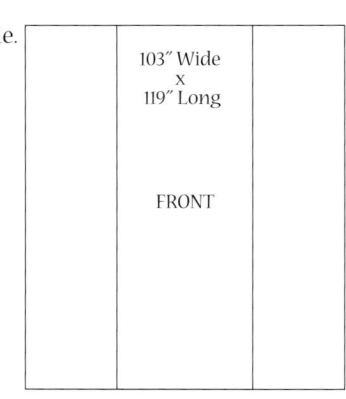

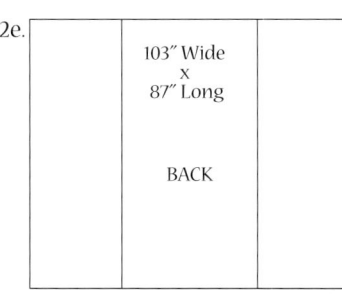

1c. Stitch / FRONT

1e. Trim / Trim to 103" Wide / FRONT / Trim

1e. 103" Wide x 119" Long / FRONT

2e. 103" Wide x 87" Long / BACK

* Continue with diagrams at top of page 7, Step 3a-e.

Cover with Contrasting Front Overlap

All Sizes

Use ½" seam allowance.

1. Cut pieces of fabric for front overlap:

Twin	2 pieces width of fabric by 29"
D/Queen	3 pieces width of fabric by 29"
King	3 pieces width of fabric by 29"

2. Cut pieces of fabric for front:

Twin	2 pieces width of fabric by 90"
D/Queen	3 pieces width of fabric by 90"
King	3 pieces width of fabric by 90"

3. Follow written directions for comforter with front and front overlap of one fabric, pages 6 and 7, Steps 1b-3f, using diagrams at right for vertical dimensions of front and front overlap.

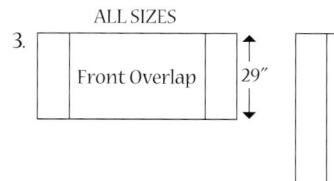

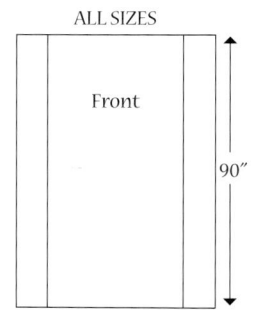

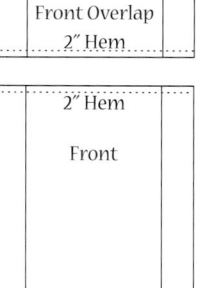

3. ALL SIZES — Front Overlap — 29"

ALL SIZES — Front — 90"

ALL SIZES — Front Overlap 2" Hem / 2" Hem Front

Quilted Comforter Cover

Photos on pages 17, 20, 52, and 56.

This style of comforter cover has a quilted top. The top is lined with a separate back to enclose the comforter, it is bound on all sides, and it has a snap tape closing at the bottom edge.

COMFORTER SIZING Comforters come in more sizes than other bedding, so we checked many stores and catalogs before deciding on dimensions to use for our directions.

By far the most common comforter length was 86", so we settled easily on that. The variations were most commonly 90", 92", and 96". If your comforter is one of those lengths, you can add 4", 6", or 10" to the lengths in our charts. Add this length in the top border where it will be less noticeable because part of it will be under the pillows, or add another row of blocks. Adjust yardage as needed.

The widths of comforters also vary. We chose one of the more common widths in each bed size. If your comforter is wider than ours, add width to the borders, adjusting border yardage as needed.

	Twin	Double/Queen	King
Purchased Comforter Width by length	64 x 86"	86 x 86"	102 x 86"

Yardage Use 42-44"-wide fabric. Allow extra if matching plaids.

See charts on pages 10, 12, 14, and 18 for yardage for the quilted fronts of the comforter covers seen on pages 17 and front cover, 20, 52, and 56. Yardage for the backing of the quilted comforter cover front will be given there. Yardage for the back of the comforter cover is given here.

	Twin	Double/Queen	King
Back	5⅜ yds.	8 yds.	8 yds.
Binding	1⅛ yds.	1¼ yds.	1⅜ yds.
Snap tape 1" wide	62"	84"	100"

All Sizes

Use ½" seam allowance.

1. Cut crossgrain strips of binding 3¾" wide (twin–8 strips, double/queen–9 strips, king–10 strips). Stitch binding strips end to end. Press in half lengthwise, wrong sides together.

2. FRONT

   a. Make quilted top referring to pages 10, 12, 14, or 18 for directions. Note: Quilt and trim, do not bind.

   b. Bind bottom edge of quilt with a ⅝" seam allowance for a wide finish.

3. BACK

   a. Follow directions on pages 4-5 for cutting and stitching back:

   Twin – Page 4 – Steps 1a-d
   Double/Queen – Page 5 – Steps 1a-d
   King – Page 5 – Steps 1a-d

   b. Hem: Press 2" to wrong side at bottom edge, then 2" to wrong side again. Stitch close to fold.

   c. Lay back on floor wrong side up. Lay quilted comforter front on top, right side up, centered from side to side, bound bottom edge just overlapping hem on back. Cut sides and top of back even with quilted front.

4. ASSEMBLE

   a. Layer back, wrong side up, then front, right side up, bound bottom edge just overlapping hem on back. Pin. Baste sides and top edge.

   b. Bind side and top edges of comforter cover using ⅝" seam allowance. Fold raw ends to inside at bottom edge before hand stitching binding to back of comforter cover.

   c. Stitch snap tape to each side of bottom opening.

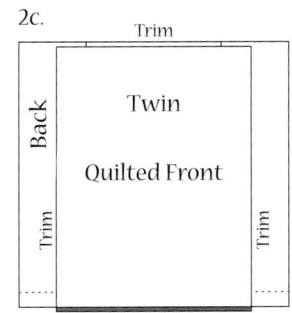

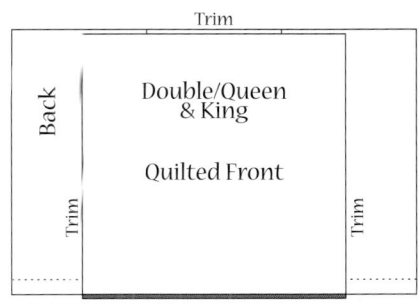

Twinkle Twinkle
Quilt or Quilted Comforter Cover

Photo on page 56.

Use 42-44"-wide fabric. When strips appear in the cutting list, cut crossgrain strips (selvage to selvage).

Backing and binding yardage given on this page is for the the quilt only. If making the comforter cover, refer to page 9 for comforter back and binding yardage and construction directions.

Yardage

TWIN – 64x86" – 9" blocks set 6x8

Background & border – white	4⅝ yds.
Stars – reds to total	3½ yds.
Backing of quilted comforter front	5⅜ yds.
Binding for quilt only, not comforter cover	¾ yd.
Batting	70x92"

DOUBLE/QUEEN – 86x86" – 9" blocks set 8x8

Background & border – white	6¼ yds.
Stars – reds to total	4¾ yds.
Backing of quilted comforter front	8 yds.
Binding for quilt only, not comforter cover	¾ yd.
Batting	92x92"

KING – 102x86" – 9" blocks set 10x8

Background & border – white	6⅞ yds.
Stars – reds to total	5½ yds.
Backing of quilted comforter front	8 yds.
Binding for quilt only, not comforter cover	⅞ yd.
Batting	108x92"

Cutting

TWIN – 48 blocks

Bkgrnd	side borders	4 strips 5½" wide
	top border	2 strips 9½" wide
	bottom border	2 strips 5½" wide
	A	96 squares – 3½"
	B	192 squares – 2"
	C	192 rectangles – 2³⁄₁₆ x 4⁵⁄₁₆"
Stars	B	384 squares – 2"
	C	192 rectangles – 2³⁄₁₆ x 4⁵⁄₁₆"
Binding		8 strips 2½" wide

DOUBLE/QUEEN – 64 blocks

Bkgrnd	side borders	4 strips 7½" wide
	top border	3 strips 7½" wide
	bottom border	3 strips 7½" wide
	A	128 squares – 3½"
	B	256 squares – 2"
	C	256 rectangles – 2³⁄₁₆ x 4⁵⁄₁₆"
Stars	B	512 squares – 2"
	C	256 rectangles – 2³⁄₁₆ x 4⁵⁄₁₆"
Binding		9 strips 2½" wide

Twin

KING – 80 blocks

Bkgrnd	side borders	4 strips 6½" wide
	top border	3 strips 8½" wide
	bottom border	3 strips 6½" wide
	A	160 squares – 3½"
	B	320 squares – 2"
	C	320 rectangles – 2³⁄₁₆ x 4⁵⁄₁₆"
Stars	B	640 squares – 2"
	C	320 rectangles – 2³⁄₁₆ x 4⁵⁄₁₆"
Binding		10 strips 2½" wide

Directions

Use ¼" seam allowance unless otherwise noted.

1. Following diagram, cut rectangles (C) in half diagonally. **Caution**: Half of the white and half of the red must be cut one direction and the other half of each color must be cut the other direction to create reversed pieces.

2. Make blocks as shown (48 for twin, 64 for double/queen, 80 for king). Press.

3. Stitch blocks into horizontal rows, rotating as shown in whole-quilt diagram above (8 rows of 6 blocks for twin, 8 rows of 8 blocks for D/Q, 8 rows of 10 blocks for king). Stitch rows together. Press.

4. **Border:** Measure length of quilt. Piece border strips cut for side borders to the measured length and stitch to sides of quilt. Repeat at top with border strips cut for top border. Repeat at bottom with border strips cut for bottom border. Press.

5. Piece backing vertically to same size as batting. Layer and quilt as desired. Trim backing and batting even with top.

6. **To Make Quilt into Comforter Cover:** Do not bind; refer to directions on page 9.

   To Bind Quilt: Stitch binding strips end to end. Press in half lengthwise, wrong sides together. Bind quilt using ⅜" seam allowance.

1.

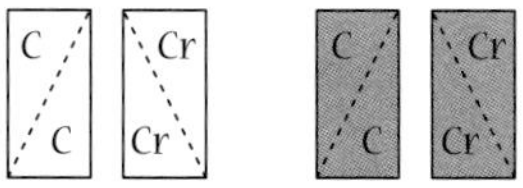

Cut half of the white rectangles one way & half the other way. Repeat with red rectangles.

2. 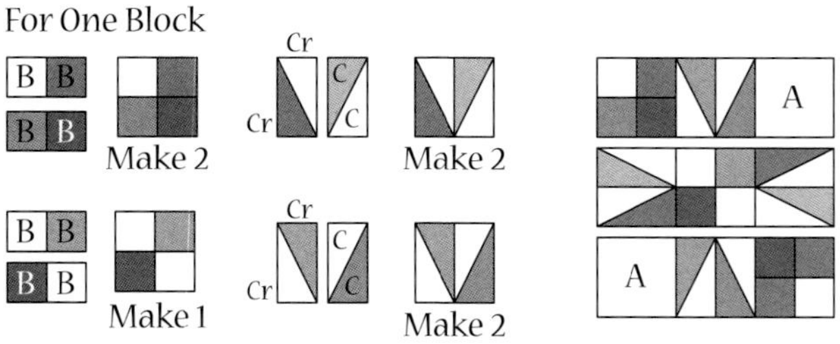 For One Block

  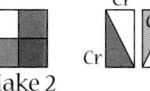 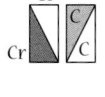 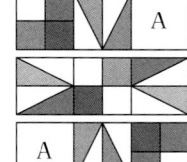

Make 2   Make 2

 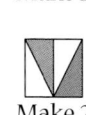

Make 1   Make 2

3.

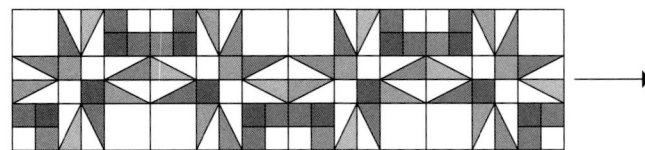

Twinkle Twinkle
Throw Pillows

Photo on page 56.

Use 42-44"-wide fabric. When strips appear in the cutting list, cut crossgrain strips (selvage to selvage).

Yardage   Makes one 20" pillow

Background & border 2 – white	⅝ yd.
Border 1 – 2 or more reds	⅛ yd. each
Backing for quilting	¾ yd.
Backing for pillow	⅞ yd.
Binding	⅓ yd.
Batting	24x24"
20" pillow form	
Red embroidery floss	

Cutting

Background – center		1 square – 12½"
	border 1	4 rectangles 2⅝ x 7⅞"
	border 2	2 rectangles 2½ x 16½"
		2 rectangles 2½ x 20½"
Reds – border 1		4 squares – 2½"
		4 rectangles 2⅝ x 7⅞"
Backing for pillow		2 pieces 20½ x 28"
Binding		2-3 strips 2½" wide

Directions

1. Following diagram, cut rectangles in half diagonally. **Caution:** Two of the white and two of the red must be cut one direction and the other two of each color must be cut the other direction to create reversed pieces.

2. Make block as shown. Press.

3. Using a light box, trace one of the baby designs on pages 54 or 55 to the block. Position lettering over and under babies, referring to photo. Lettering for Good Night is on page 51. Embroider with a stem or back stitch using two strands of red floss.

4. Cut backing for quilting the same size as batting. Layer and quilt as desired. Trim backing and batting even with top.

5. Press pieces for pillow back in half, wrong sides together, to 20½ x 14". Pin one piece to wrong side of pillow top, raw edges even. Pin other piece on top of first one, raw edges even, folded edges overlapping in center. Baste outside edge.

6. Stitch binding strips end to end. Press in half lengthwise, wrong sides together. Bind using ⅜" seam allowance. Insert pillow form.

1.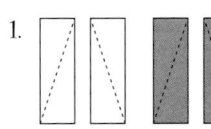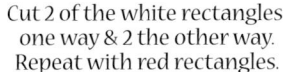

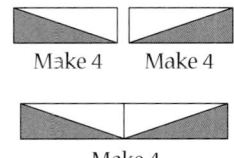

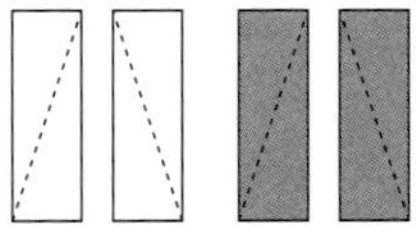

Cut 2 of the white rectangles one way & 2 the other way. Repeat with red rectangles.

Make 4   Make 4

Make 4

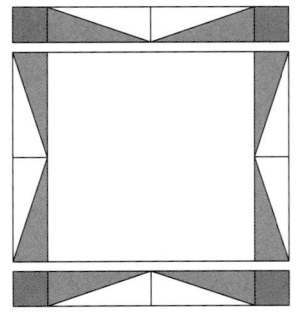 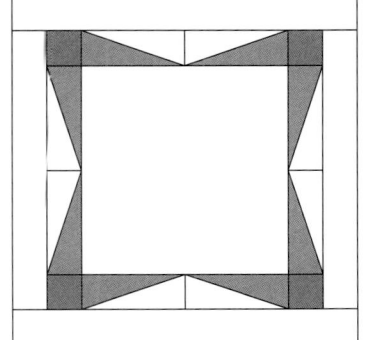

Garden Path
Quilt or Quilted Comforter Cover

Photo on page 52. Use 42-44"-wide fabric.

Backing and binding yardage given on this page is for the the quilt only. If making the comforter cover, refer to page 9 for comforter back and binding yardage and construction directions.

Yardage

TWIN - 64x86"

Background – light tan	2¼ yds.
Bars – prints to total	2⅝ yds.
Appliques – flower – red	⅞ yd.
flower center – gold	⅛ yd.
leaf & vine – green	1 yd.
Border – red print	2¼ yds.
Backing of quilted comforter front	5⅜ yds.
Binding for quilt only, not comforter cover	¾ yd.
Batting	70x92"

DOUBLE/QUEEN - 86x86"

Background – light tan	2¼ yds.
Bars – prints to total	3 yds.
Appliques – flower – red	1¼ yds.
flower center – gold	⅛ yd.
leaf & vine – green	1¼ yds.
Border – red print	2¾ yds.
Backing of quilted comforter front	8 yds.
Binding for quilt only, not comforter cover	¾ yd.
Batting	92x92"

KING - 102x86"

Background – light tan	4¼ yds.
Bars – prints to total	3½ yds.
Appliques – flower – red	1½ yds.
flower center – gold	⅛ yd.
leaf & vine – green	1½ yds.
Border – red print	3⅛ yds.
Backing of quilted comforter front	8 yds.
Binding for quilt only, not comforter cover	⅞ yd.
Batting	108x92"

Cutting Patterns on pages 62 & 66

TWIN - 4 rows bars, 3 rows applique
Background cut on lengthwise grain
           3 rectangles – 9½x72½"
Bars   192 rectangles – 2x6½"
Appliques   see Step 1a of directions
Border cut on lengthwise grain
        sides   2 rectangles – 7x72½"
   top & bottom   2 rectangles – 7½x64½"
Binding   8 strips 2½" wide

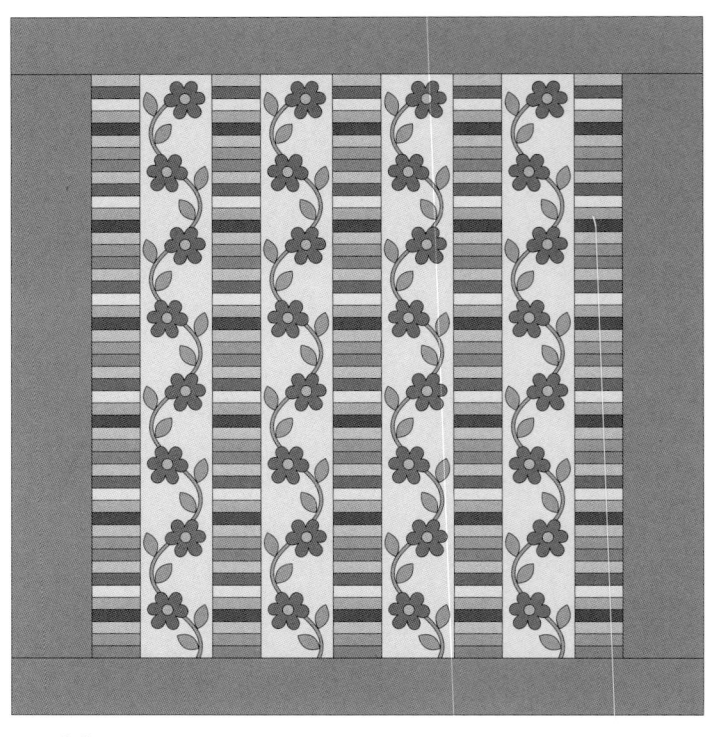

Double/Queen

DOUBLE/QUEEN - 5 rows bars, 4 rows applique
Background cut on lengthwise grain
           4 rectangles – 9½x72½"
Bars   240 rectangles – 2x6½"
Appliques   see Step 1a of directions
Border cut on lengthwise grain
        sides   2 rectangles – 10½x72½"
   top & bottom   2 rectangles – 7½x86½"
Binding   9 strips 2½" wide

KING - 6 rows bars, 5 rows applique
Background cut on lengthwise grain
           5 rectangles – 9½x72½"
Bars   288 rectangles – 2x6½"
Appliques   see Step 1a of directions
Border cut on lengthwise grain
        sides   2 rectangles – 11x72½"
   top & bottom   2 rectangles – 7½x102½"
Binding   10 strips 2½" wide

Directions

Use ¼" seam allowance unless otherwise noted.

1. Applique Rows:

    a. Trace to fusible web:

        Twin – 24 flowers/centers, 48 leaves,
           24 vine segments
        D/Queen – 32 flowers/centers, 64 leaves,
           32 vine segments
        King – 40 flowers/centers, 80 leaves,
           40 vine segments

    b. Fuse to desired fabrics and cut out.

c. Fuse vine segments to background rectangles using diagram for placement.

d. Fuse 8 flowers and 16 leaves along vine as shown, covering seams in vine with flowers. Stitch in place with machine zigzag or buttonhole stitch.

2. For each row of bars, stitch 48 rectangles together. See cutting charts for number of rows. Press.

3. Stitch alternating rows of applique and bars together. Press.

4. Border: Measure length of quilt. Trim pieces cut for side borders, if necessary, to the measured length and stitch to sides of quilt. Repeat at top and bottom with border strips cut for top and bottom borders. press.

5. Piece backing vertically to same size as batting. Layer and quilt as desired. Trim backing and batting even with top.

6. To Make Quilt into Comforter Cover: Do not bind; refer to directions on page 9.

To Bind Quilt: Stitch binding strips end to end. Press in half lengthwise, wrong sides together. Bind quilt using ⅜" seam allowance.

1c.
All Sizes
← 9½" →
5"
1½"
← 1½"
72½"
← 1½"
1½"
Trim

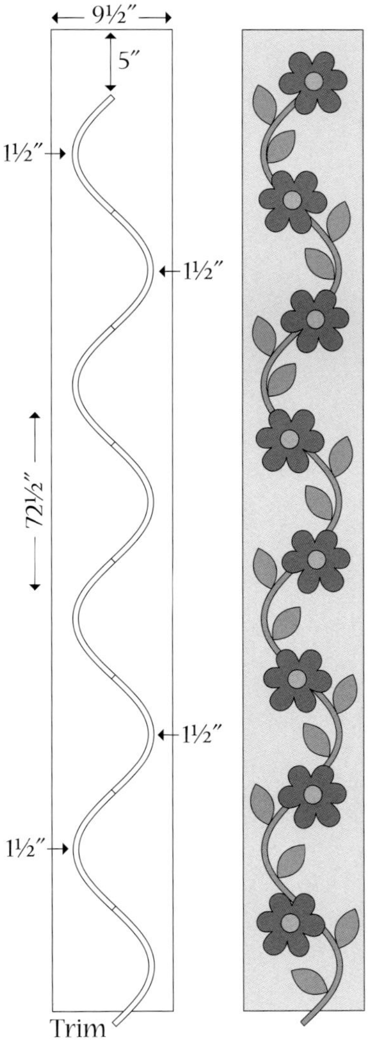

Garden Path
Pillow Covers

Photo on page 52. Envelope back, bound edges.

Use 42-44"-wide fabric. When strips appear in cutting list, cut crossgrain strips (selvage to selvage).

Yardage   Makes 2

	STANDARD	QUEEN	KING
	20x26"	20x30"	20x36"
Background – light tan	1¼ yds.	1¼ yds.	1¼ yds.
Squares – prints to total	¼ yd.	¼ yd.	⅜ yd.
Appliques – flower – red	¼ yd.	¼ yd.	¼ yd.
center – gold	⅛ yd.	⅛ yd.	⅛ yd.
leaf & vine – green	⅜ yd.	⅜ yd.	⅜ yd.
Binding	½ yd.	½ yd.	⅝ yd.
Backing for quilting	1½ yds.	1½ yds.	1½ yds.
Back for pillow covers	2⅝ yds.	2⅝ yds.	2¾ yds.
Batting – 2 pieces	24x30"	24x34"	24x40"

Cutting   Patterns on pages 62 & 66

	STANDARD	QUEEN	KING
Background – 4 pieces	4½x27"	4½x31"	4½x37"
2 pieces	10x27"	10x31"	10x37"
Squares – 2x2"	36	42	50
Appliques – flower & center	6 each	6 each	8 each
leaf	12	14	18
vine segment	8	8	10
Back/pillow covers – 4 pieces	21x31"	21x35"	21x41"
Binding – 2½" strips	6	6	7

Directions   Diagrams on page 51

Use ¼" seam allowance unless otherwise noted.

1. Stitch 2" squares into 2 rows of equal length. Stitch to either side of large background rectangle. Stitch other background rectangles to sides. Trim excess from squares rows if needed.

2. Applique

   a. Trace appliques to fusible web. Fuse to desired fabrics and cut out.

   b. Fuse vine segments to center panel of pillow cover, trimming ends where shown. See diagram on page 51.

   c. Fuse flowers and leaves along vine, making sure to cover joins in vine. Machine zigzag or buttonhole stitch.

3. Cut backing (for quilting) to same size as batting. Layer and quilt as desired. Trim backing and batting even with top.

4. Press pieces for pillow backs in half crosswise, wrong sides together. Pin one piece to wrong side of pillow top, raw edges even. Pin other piece on top of first one, raw edges even, folded edges overlapping in center. Baste outside edge.

5. Stitch binding strips end to end. Press in half lengthwise, wrong sides together. Bind pillow covers using ⅜" seam allowance.

13

Country Traditions
Quilt or Quilted Comforter Cover

Photo on page 17.

Use 42-44"-wide fabric. When strips appear in the cutting list, cut crossgrain strips (selvage to selvage).

Backing and binding yardage given on this page is for the the quilt only. If making the comforter cover, refer to page 9 for comforter back and binding yardage and construction directions.

Yardage

TWIN – 64x86"

Squares – prints to total	4⅝ yds.
Border	1¾ yds.
Backing of quilted comforter front	5⅜ yds.
Binding for quilt only, not comforter cover	¾ yd.
Batting	70x92"

DOUBLE/QUEEN – 86x86"

Squares – prints to total	6 yds.
Border	2⅓ yds.
Backing of quilted comforter front	8 yds.
Binding for quilt only, not comforter cover	¾ yd.
Batting	92x92"

KING – 102x86"

Squares – prints to total	7¼ yds.
Border	2¼ yds.
Backing of quilted comforter front	8 yds.
Binding for quilt only, not comforter cover	⅞ yd.
Batting	108x92"

Cutting

TWIN – 432 squares set 18x24

Squares		432 squares – 3½"
Border	sides	4 strips 5½" wide
	bottom	2 strips 5½" wide
	top	2 strips 9½" wide
Binding		8 strips 2½" wide

DOUBLE/QUEEN – 576 squares set 24x24

Squares		576 squares – 3½"
Border	sides	4 strips 7½" wide
	bottom	3 strips 7½" wide
	top	3 strips 7½" wide
Binding		9 strips 2½" wide

KING – 720 squares set 30x24

Squares		720 squares – 3½"
Border	sides	4 strips 6½" wide
	bottom	3 strips 6½" wide
	top	3 strips 8½" wide
Binding		10 strips 2½" wide

Twin

Directions

Use ¼" seam allowance unless otherwise noted.

1. Stitch squares into horizontal rows:

    Twin – 24 rows of 18 squares each
    Double/Queen – 24 rows of 24 squares each
    King – 24 rows of 30 squares each

2. Stitch rows together. Press.

3. Border: Measure length of quilt. Piece border strips cut for side borders to the measured length and stitch to sides of quilt. Repeat at bottom with border strips cut for bottom border. Repeat at top with border strips cut for top border. Press.

4. Piece backing vertically to same size as batting. Layer and quilt as desired. Trim backing and batting even with top.

5. To Make Quilt into Comforter Cover: Do not bind; refer to directions on page 9.

    To Bind Quilt: Stitch binding strips end to end. Press in half lengthwise, wrong sides together. Bind quilt using ⅜" seam allowance.

Country Traditions
Pillow Covers

Photo on page 17. Open end, bound edges.

Use 42-44"-wide fabric. When strips appear in cutting list, cut crossgrain strips (selvage to selvage).

Yardage Makes 2

	STANDARD	QUEEN	KING
	20x30"	20x34"	20x40"
Main fabric	1⅝ yds.	1⅞ yds.	2¼ yds.
Squares – 7-14 prints	⅛ yd. ea.	⅛ yd. ea.	⅛ yd. ea.
Narrow border	¼ yd.	¼ yd.	¼ yd.
Backing for quilting	3 yds.	3 yds.	5⅛ yds.
Binding	¾ yd.	¾ yd.	⅞ yd.
Batting – 4 pieces	24x34"	24x38"	24x44"

Cutting

	STANDARD	QUEEN	KING
Main fabric – 4 pieces	3¼ x 21"	3¼ x 21"	3¼ x 21"
4 pieces	21x21"	21x25"	21x31"
Squares – 3½"	56	56	56
Narrow border – 1" strips	5	5	5
Binding – 3" strips	7	7	8

Directions

Use ¼" seam allowance unless otherwise noted.

1. Make 4 sets of patchwork as shown. Stitch 1" strips to both sides of each set. Stitch narrow background piece to one side and wide background piece to the other side. Make four. Press.

2. Cut backing to same size as batting. Layer and quilt as desired. Trim backing and batting even with top.

3. Stitch binding strips end to end. Press in half lengthwise, wrong sides together. Bind end of each piece closest to patchwork using ½" seam allowance.

4. Pin two pillow cover pieces wrong sides together. Bind remaining end and the two sides using ½" seam allowance.

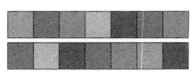 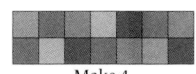

Make 4

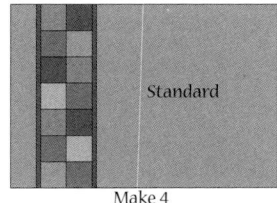

Standard

Make 4

 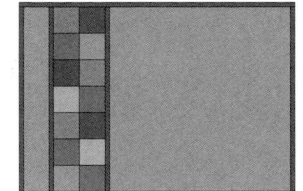

Bind end of each piece

Bind other 3 sides

Country Traditions
Throw Pillows

Photo on page 17.

Use 42-44"-wide fabric. When strips appear in cutting list, cut crossgrain strips (selvage to selvage).

Yardage Makes one 18" pillow

Background	⅝ yd.
Appliques – hearts	⅙ yd.
tulip sides	⅙ yd.
tulip centers	⅛ yd.
leaves & stems	⅛ yd.
Backing for quilting	¾ yd.
Backing for pillow	1¼ yds.
Binding	¼ yd.
Batting	22x22"
18" pillow form	

Cutting Patterns on page 59

Background	1 square – 18½"
Appliques	4 each
Backing for pillow	2 pieces 18½x22"
Binding	2 strips 2½" wide

Directions

1. Applique hearts and flowers to background square.

2. Cut backing for quilting the same size as batting. Layer and quilt as desired. Trim backing and batting even with top.

3. Press pieces for pillow back in half, wrong sides together, to 18½ x 11". Pin one piece to wrong side of pillow top, raw edges even. Pin other piece on top of first one, raw edges even, folded edges overlapping in center. Baste outside edge.

4. Stitch binding strips end to end. Press in half lengthwise wrong sides together. Bind using ⅜" seam allowance. Insert pillow form.

Country Traditions
Topper

Photo on page 17.

Approximate finished size 51"

25½" block – set 2x2

Use 42-44"-wide fabric. When strips appear in the cutting list, cut crossgrain strips (selvage to selvage).

Yardage

Background	1⅞ yds.
Nine-patch blocks – lights	¾ yd.
darks	1 yd.
Appliques – hearts	½ yd.
tulips	⅓ yd.
tulip centers	⅙ yd.
leaves & stems	⅛ yd.
Backing	3⅜ yds.
Binding	½ yd.
Batting	55x55"

Cutting   Patterns on page 59

Background	center squares	29 squares – 6½"
	side triangles	5 squares – 9¾"
	corner triangles	2 squares – 5⅛"
Nine-patches	lights	128 squares – 2½"
	darks	160 squares – 2½"
Appliques		16 each
Binding		6 strips 2½" wide

Directions

Use ¼" seam allowance unless otherwise noted.

1. Make 32 nine-patch blocks as shown.

2. Cut 9¾" background squares for sides in **quarters** diagonally. Cut 5⅛" background squares for corners in **half** diagonally.

3. Stitch diagonal rows of corner triangles, side triangles, nine-patch blocks, and center squares, as shown. Stitch rows together. Press.

4. Place appliques as shown. Machine zigzag or buttonhole stitch in place.

5. Piece backing to same size as batting. Layer and quilt as desired. Trim backing and batting even with top.

6. Stitch binding strips end to end. Press in half lengthwise, wrong sides together. Bind quilt using ⅜" seam allowance.

1.
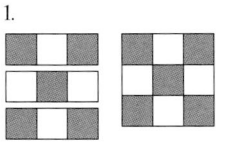

2.
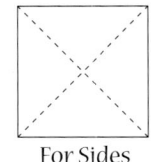

For Sides

For Corners

3.

4.
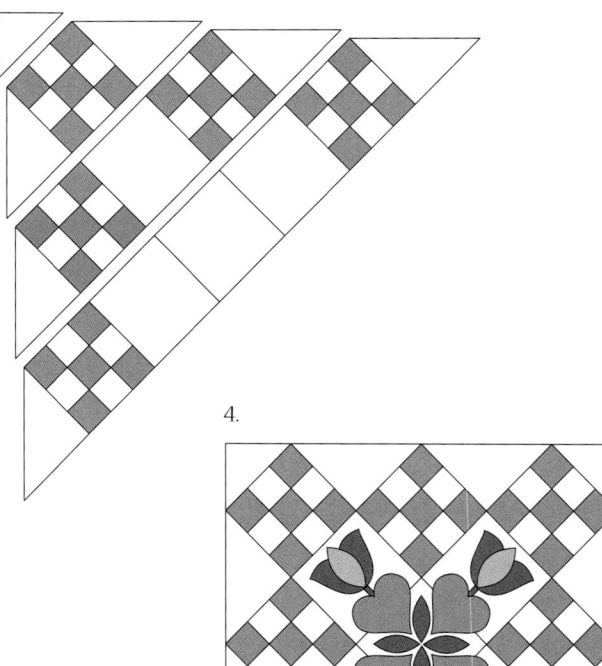

Country Traditions Quilted Comforter Cover, Topper, Pillow Covers, and Throw Pillows   **17**

See photo index page 3

Happy Hearts
Quilt or Quilted Comforter Cover

Photo on page 20.

Use 42-44"-wide fabric. When strips appear in the cutting list, cut crossgrain strips (selvage to selvage).

Backing and binding yardage given on this page is for the the quilt only. If making the comforter cover, refer to page 9 for comforter back and binding yardage and construction directions.

Yardage

TWIN – 64x86"

Squares – prints to total	3¾ yds.
Hearts – 3 prints	⅓ yd. each
Border	2⅛ yds.
Backing of quilted comforter front	5⅜ yds.
Binding for quilt only, not comforter cover	¾ yd.
Batting	70x92"

DOUBLE/QUEEN – 86x86"

Squares – prints to total	6 yds.
Hearts – 5 prints	⅓ yd. each
Border	2¼ yds.
Backing of quilted comforter front	8 yds.
Binding for quilt only, not comforter cover	¾ yd.
Batting	92x92"

KING – 102x86"

Squares – prints to total	6½ yds.
Hearts – 6 prints	⅓ yd. each
Border	2¼ yds.
Backing of quilted comforter front	8 yds.
Binding for quilt only, not comforter cover	⅞ yd.
Batting	108x92"

Cutting   Heart pattern on page 79

TWIN – 54 squares set 6x9

Squares		54 squares – 8½"
Hearts		9
Border	sides	4 strips 8½" wide
	bottom	2 strips 8½" wide
	top	2 strips 6½" wide
Binding		8 strips 2½" wide

DOUBLE/QUEEN – 81 squares set 9x9

Squares		81 squares – 8½"
Hearts		15
Border	sides	4 strips 7½" wide
	bottom	3 strips 7½" wide
	top	3 strips 7½" wide
Binding		9 strips 2½" wide

KING – 99 squares set 11x9

Squares		99 squares – 8½"
Hearts		18

Double/Queen

Border	sides	4 strips 7½" wide
	bottom	3 strips 7½" wide
	top	3 strips 7½" wide
Binding		10 strips 2½" wide

Directions

Use ¼" seam allowance unless otherwise noted.

1. Stitch squares into horizontal rows:

   Twin – 9 rows of 6 squares each
   Double/Queen – 9 rows of 9 squares each
   King – 9 rows of 11 squares each

2. Stitch rows together. Press.

3. Border: Measure length of quilt. Piece border strips cut for side borders to the measured length and stitch to sides of quilt. Repeat at bottom with border strips cut for bottom border. Repeat at top with border strips cut for top border. Press.

4. Applique hearts to double/queen quilt top in 3 staggered rows of 5 as shown in whole-quilt diagram. For twin, make 3 staggered rows of 3 hearts. For king, make 3 staggered rows of 6 hearts.

5. Piece backing vertically to same size as batting. Layer and quilt as desired. Trim backing and batting even with top.

6. To Make Quilt into Comforter Cover: Do not bind; refer to directions on page 9.

   To Bind Quilt: Stitch binding strips end to end. Press in half lengthwise, wrong sides together. Bind quilt using ⅜" seam allowance.

Match to dotted line on top piece for full-sized pattern

Happy Hearts
Throw Pillow

Photo on page 20.

Use 42-44"-wide fabric.

Yardage   Makes 1

Fabric   ⅝ yd.
Flannel – white – lining   ⅝ yd.
Fiberfill   1#

Cutting

Heart   2
Flannel   2 rectangles 20x20"

Directions

Use ¼" seam allowance.

1. Pin heart pieces wrong sides together with flannel lining pieces. Machine baste close to edge of heart. Cut excess flannel away.

2. Place lined heart pieces right sides together and stitch around outside, leaving 4" open on one side for turning. Clip. Turn.

3. Stuff firmly with fiberfill.

4. Stitch opening closed.

Match to dotted line on lower piece for full-sized pattern

19

Happy Hearts Quilted Comforter Cover, Throw Pillows, and Pillowcases
See photo index page 3

Denim Blues Overlap Comforter Cover, Topper, Pillow Covers, T-Shirt and Denim Throw Pillows 21

See photo index page 3

Denim Blues
Topper

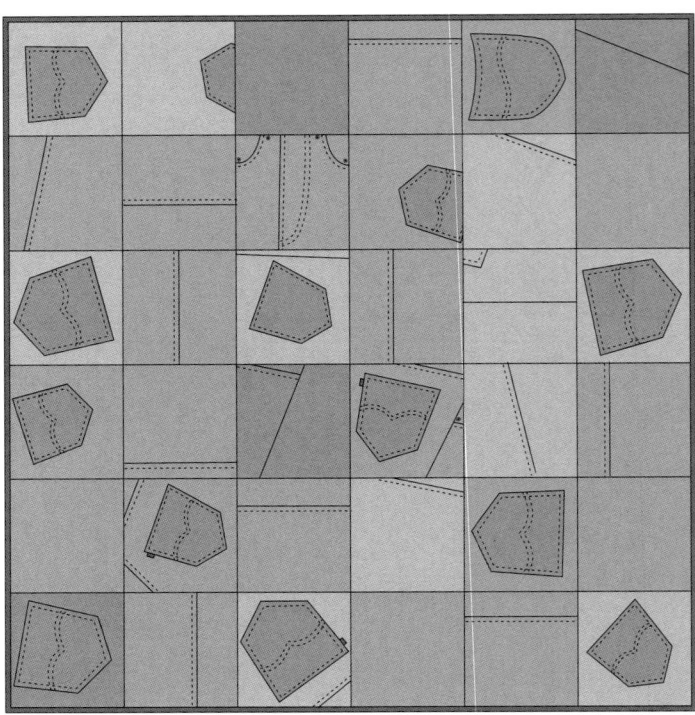

Photo on page 21. Made from old jeans. No batting.

Approximate finished size 48"

8" block – set 6x6

Use 42-44"-wide fabric. When strips appear in the cutting list, cut crossgrain strips (selvage to selvage).

Yardage

Blocks	old jeans
Backing	3⅛ yds.
Binding	½ yd. (a bandanna print is nice)

Cutting

Blocks	36 squares – 8½" – cut over pocket or other interesting seamed areas
Binding	5 strips 2½" wide

Directions

Use ¼" seam allowance unless otherwise noted.

1. Stitch squares into 6 horizontal rows of 6 blocks.

2. Stitch rows together. Press.

3. Piece backing to 52" square. Layer top and backing. Stitch together along seams between blocks. Trim backing even with top.

4. Stitch binding strips end to end. Press in half lengthwise, wrong sides together. Bind using ⅜" seam allowance.

5. Embellish with bandanna in one of the pockets, if desired.

Denim Blues Throw Pillows
T-Shirt Throw Pillows

Photo on page 21.

Supplies

Front & back	1 T-shirt
Medium-weight woven or nonwoven fusible interfacing (not knit)	1 yd.
Fiberfill	1-2#

Directions

1. Lay T-shirt on table and smooth out both front and back.

2. Determine design area to be used. Do not include armhole or neckline seams in this measurement.

3. Draw a square including ¼" seam allowance. Cut out front and back at the same time.

4. Cut interfacing pieces the same size as front and back. Following manufacturer's directions, fuse interfacing to wrong side of pillow squares. Do not stretch T-shirt fabric.

5. Place front and back right sides together and stitch around outside, leaving 4" open for turning.

6. Clip. Turn right side out. Stuff firmly with fiberfill. Stitch opening closed.

Denim Throw Pillows

Photo on page 21.

Supplies

jeans or denim shirt	
muslin (1 pillow)	1 yd.
fiberfill (1 pillow)	1-2#

Directions Jeans Pillow

1. Lay jeans right side up on table and cut across just above crotch level. Turn wrong side out.

2. Refold so side seams line up. Pin side seams together.

3. With a straightedge, draw center front and center back seamlines on both sides. On the front the stitching line will start near the base of the fly, and on the back it will start near the

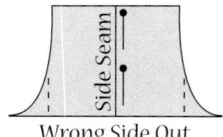

Wrong Side Out

base of the yoke. Pin and stitch center front and center back seams.

4. Refold jeans so bottom raw edges line up. Pin and stitch bottom seam. Turn right side out.

5. Line up waistband edges and topstitch across top of pillow.

6. Make a pillow form the same size as the pillow with muslin and fiberfill. Put form into pillow through fly.

Directions   Denim Shirt Pillow

1. Button shirt, turn wrong side out, and lay flat on table with front up. Smooth all wrinkles out of front and back.

2. With a straight-edge, draw a straight line from the shoulder to the desired length, avoiding buttons/button-holes. Pin.

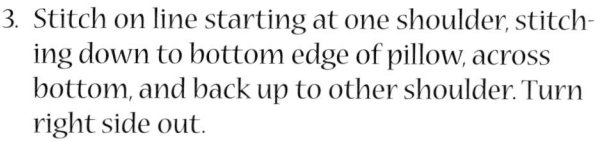

Wrong Side Out

3. Stitch on line starting at one shoulder, stitching down to bottom edge of pillow, across bottom, and back up to other shoulder. Turn right side out.

4. Cut a 6" square from shirt scraps. Pin into neckline and invisibly hand stitch in place.

5. Make a pillow form the same size as the pillow with muslin and fiberfill. Put form into pillow through shirt opening.

Denim Blues
Pillow Covers

Photo on page 21. Envelope front, turned edges.

Use 42-44"-wide fabric. When strips appear in cutting list, cut crossgrain strips (selvage to selvage).

Yardage   Makes 2

	STANDARD	QUEEN	KING
	20x26"	20x30"	20x36"
Front & back – plaid	1¾ yds.	2 yds.	2⅜ yds.
Front overlaps – denim	1 yd.	1⅛ yds.	1⅜ yds.
⅞" buttons	12	12	12
Velcro® dots, large, self adhesive	12	12	12

Cutting

	STANDARD	QUEEN	KING
Front – plaid – 2 pieces	21x25"	21x29"	21x35"
Back – plaid – 2 pieces	21x28"	21x32"	21x38"
Front overlaps – 4 pieces	21x15"	21x17"	21x21"

Directions

1. Make 1" double hem on both 21" sides of front. (Press 1" to wrong side then 1" again. Stitch along fold.)

2. Press front overlaps in half, wrong sides together, to: 21x7½" for twin, 21x8½" for queen, 21x10½" for king.

3. Lay backing on table, right side up. Lay one front overlap on each end, raw edges even. Lay front on top, centered, right side down. See diagram. Stitch around entire outside edge with a ½" seam allowance. Clip corners. Turn.

4. Stitch 3 buttons to side of each overlap, approximately 5" apart. Stick loop halves of Velcro® dots on front overlap under each button and hook halves on front under each button.

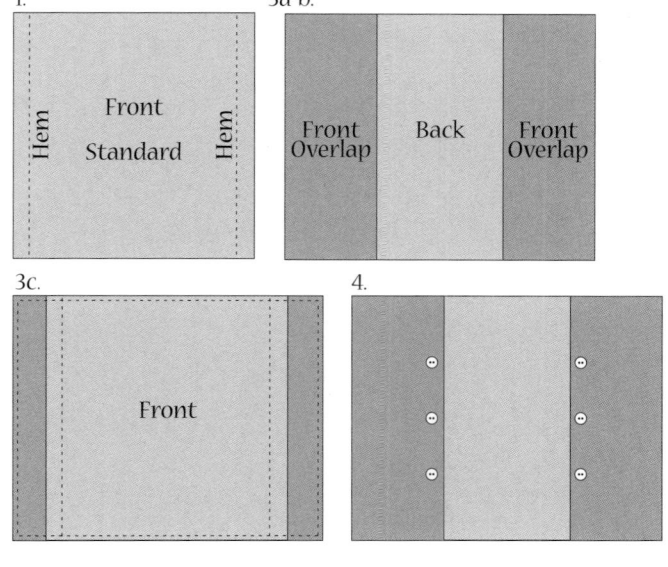

1.

| Hem | Front Standard | Hem |

3a-b.

| Front Overlap | Back | Front Overlap |

3c.

Front

4.

24   **Paint Box Plaids Topper and Throw Pillow**
See photo index page 3

NorthWoods Topper, Traditional Comforter Cover, Pillow Covers, and Pillowcases   25

NorthWoods
Topper

Photo on page 25.

Approximate finished size 64"

8" block – set 8x8

Use 42-44"-wide fabric. When strips appear in the cutting list, cut crossgrain strips (selvage to selvage).

Yardage

Blocks – flannels to total	4½ yds.
Appliques – moon – gold	¼ yd.
moose – brown	½ yd.
antlers – tan	¼ yd.
tree – 5 greens	⅛-¼ yd. each
tree trunk – brown	scrap
Backing	4⅛ yds.
Binding	⅝ yd.
Batting	70x70"

Cutting   Patterns on pages 72, 73, 75

Blocks	64 squares – 8½"
Appliques	1 each
Binding	7 strips 2½" wide

Directions

Use ¼" seam allowance unless otherwise noted.

1. Stitch squares into 8 horizontal rows of 8 blocks.

2. Stitch rows together. Press.

3. Place appliques on quilt top as shown in whole-quilt diagram. Machine zigzag or buttonhole stitch.

4. Piece backing to same size as batting. Layer and quilt as desired. Trim backing and batting even with top.

5. Stitch binding strips end to end. Press in half lengthwise, wrong sides together. Bind quilt using ⅜" seam allowance.

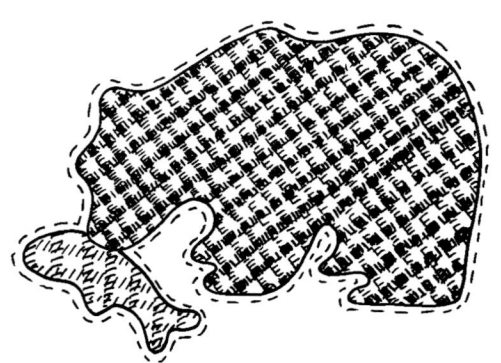

NorthWoods
Pillow Covers

Photo on page 25. Open end, turned edges.

Use 42-44"-wide fabric. When strips appear in cutting list, cut crossgrain strips (selvage to selvage).

Yardage   Makes 2

	STANDARD	QUEEN	KING
	20x30"	20x34"	20x40"
Main fabric – tan plaid	2 yds.	2¼ yds.	2½ yds.
Appliques – 3-6 greens,			
2-3 browns, 2 golds	⅓ yd. ea.	⅓ yd. ea.	⅓ yd. ea.
sky, mountains,			
hills, beach	½ yd. ea.	½ yd. ea.	½ yd. ea.
water	⅓ yd. ea.	⅓ yd. ea.	⅓ yd. ea.
Binding	⅓ yd.	⅓ yd.	⅓ yd.
Backing for quilting	2¾ yds.	2¾ yds.	2¾ yds.
Batting – 2 pieces	45x34"	45x38"	45x44"

Cutting   Patterns on pages 72, 74, 75, 76, 77, 78, 79

	STANDARD	QUEEN	KING
Main fabric – 2 pieces	30½ x 42"	34½ x 42"	40½ x 42"
Appliques – 2 each of sky,			
mountains, hills, beach	7x30½"	7x34½"	7x40½"
water – 2 pieces	4x30½"	4x34½"	4x40½"
all others as desired			
Binding – 2½" strips	2-3	2-3	2-3

Standard

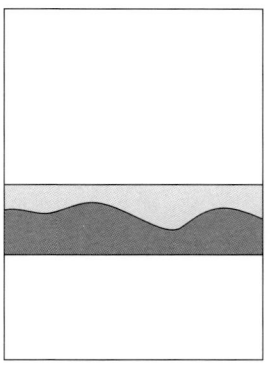
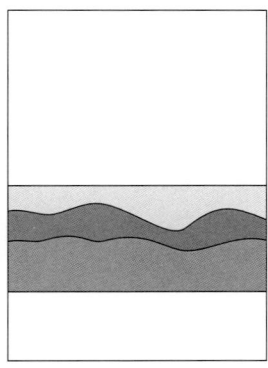

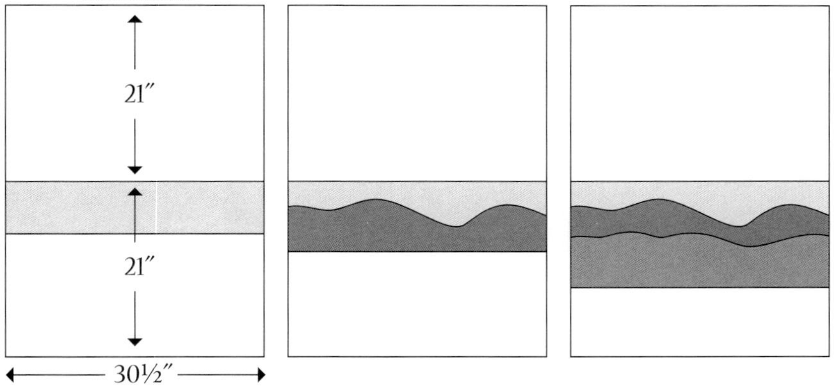

21"

21"

30½"

Directions

Use ¼" seam allowance unless otherwise noted.

1. Applique

   a. Fuse rectangles of sky, mountain, hill, beach, and water fabrics that will allow cutting out of pieces in cutting chart. Cut out rectangles listed for each fabric.

   b. Cut top edges of mountain, hill, beach, and water fabrics in wavy lines, referring to diagrams, making sure to leave ample height in each piece for overlapping.

   c. Following diagram, fuse sky rectangle to main fabric rectangle. Repeat for mountain, beach, and water rectangles, overlapping bottom edge of previous piece.

   d. Fuse remaining appliques to pillow covers, using diagrams as a guide. Machine zigzag or buttonhole stitch.

2. Cut backing to same size as batting. Layer and quilt as desired. Trim backing and batting even with top.

3. Fold in half, right sides together. Stitch side and end with ½" seam allowance. Clip corner and turn. Note: Stitch opposite end on second pillow cover so open ends of covers are opposite.

4. Stitch binding strips end to end, if necessary, to make strip long enough to fit. Press in half lengthwise, wrong sides together. Bind pillow covers using ⅜" seam allowance.

Standard

Bind

Bind

Sunny Days Star and Sunny Days Log Cabin Toppers, Throw Pillows, and Pillowcases
See photo index page 3

Sunny Days Star Topper   29

See photo index page 3

Sunny Days Log Cabin
Topper

Photo on page 28.

Approximate finished size 42x60"

9" block – set 4x6

Use 42-44"-wide fabric. When strips appear in the cutting list, cut crossgrain strips (selvage to selvage).

Yardage

Block centers – blue	¼ yd.
Logs – light – yellows to total	1¾ yds.
dark – blues to total	1¾ yds.
Border	¾ yd.
Backing	2⅞ yds.
Binding	½ yd.
Batting	46x66"

Cutting

Blocks	centers (blue)	24 squares – 2½"
	logs (yellow)	32-34 strips 1⅜" wide
	logs (blue)	32-34 strips 1⅜" wide
Border		6 strips 3½" wide
Binding		6 strips 2½" wide

Directions

Use ¼" seam allowance unless otherwise noted.

1. Make 24 blocks by stitching strips to center squares in four clockwise rounds. Strips 1 and 2 are light, strips 3 and 4 are dark. After stitching each strip to block, trim off remaining end of strip. See diagram. Press.

   Note: To make all blocks consistent in size, it is best to cut logs for last two rounds to the same length for all blocks. After two rounds of logs are stitched to all 24 blocks, measure several blocks to get an average length to cut the next log. Cut 24 logs that length and stitch one to each block. Repeat for remaining 7 logs. All blocks will be exactly the same size and will be much easier to stitch into rows.

2. Stitch blocks into 6 rows of 4, rotating as shown.

3. Stitch rows together. Press.

4. Border: Measure length of quilt. Piece border strips to the measured length and stitch to sides of quilt. Repeat at top and bottom. Press.

5. Piece backing horizontally to same size as batting. Layer and quilt as desired. Trim backing and batting even with top.

6. Stitch binding strips end to end. Press in half lengthwise, wrong sides together. Bind quilt using ⅜" seam allowance.

1.

Round 1

Round 2

Round 3

Round 4

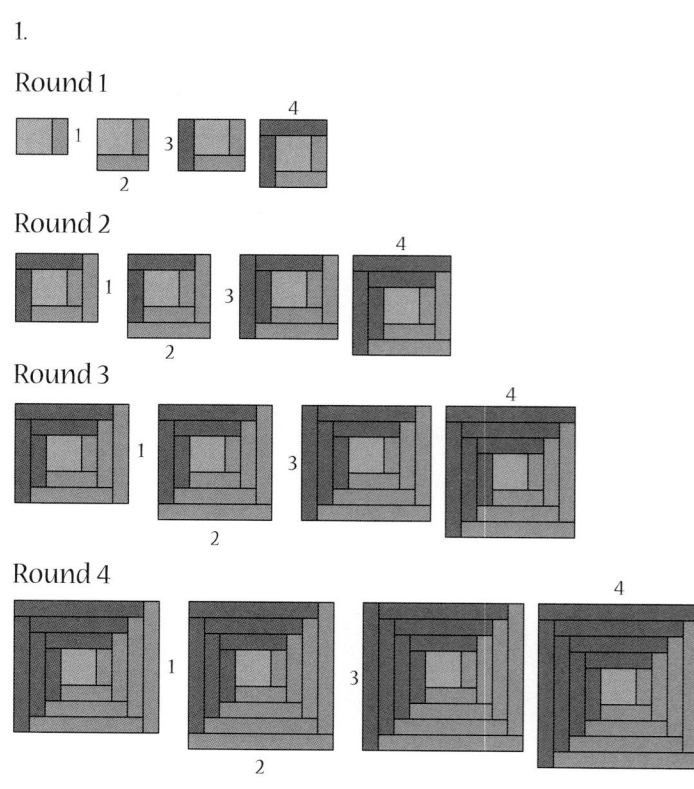

2.

Odd Rows

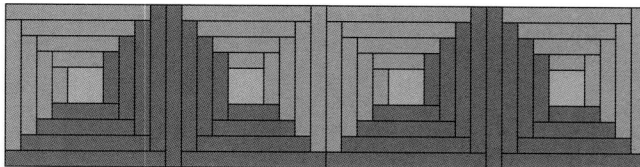

Even Rows

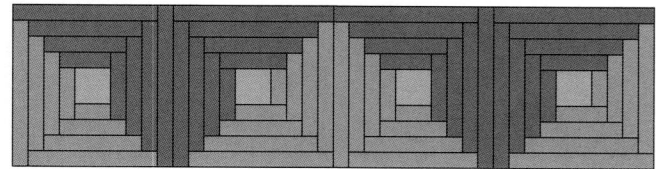

5. Stitch binding strips end to end. Press in half lengthwise, wrong sides together. Bind using ⅜″ seam allowance. Insert pillow form.

Sunny Days Log Cabin
Throw Pillow

Photo on page 28.

Use 42-44″-wide fabric. When strips appear in the cutting list, cut crossgrain strips (selvage to selvage).

Yardage Makes one 18″ pillow

Block centers – blue	⅛ yd.
Logs – light – 8 yellows	⅛ yd. each
dark – 8 blues	⅛ yd. each
Backing for quilting	¾ yd.
Backing for pillow	¾ yd.
Binding	¼ yd.
Batting	22 x 22″
18″ pillow form	

Cutting

Blocks	centers (blue)	4 squares – 2½″
	logs (yellow)	8 strips 1⅜″ wide
	logs (blue)	8 strips 1⅜″ wide
Backing for pillow		2 pieces 18½ x 22″
Binding		2 strips 2½″ wide

Directions

1. Make 4 blocks using diagrams and directions on page 30.

2. Stitch blocks together in 2 rows of 2 blocks. Place darks at center or lights at center. Press.

3. Cut backing for quilting the same size as batting. Layer and quilt as desired. Trim backing and batting even with top.

4. Press 18½ x 22″ pieces for envelope back in half, wrong sides together, to 18½ x 11″. Place both pieces on wrong side of pillow top, matching raw edges and overlapping folded edges in center. Baste outside edge.

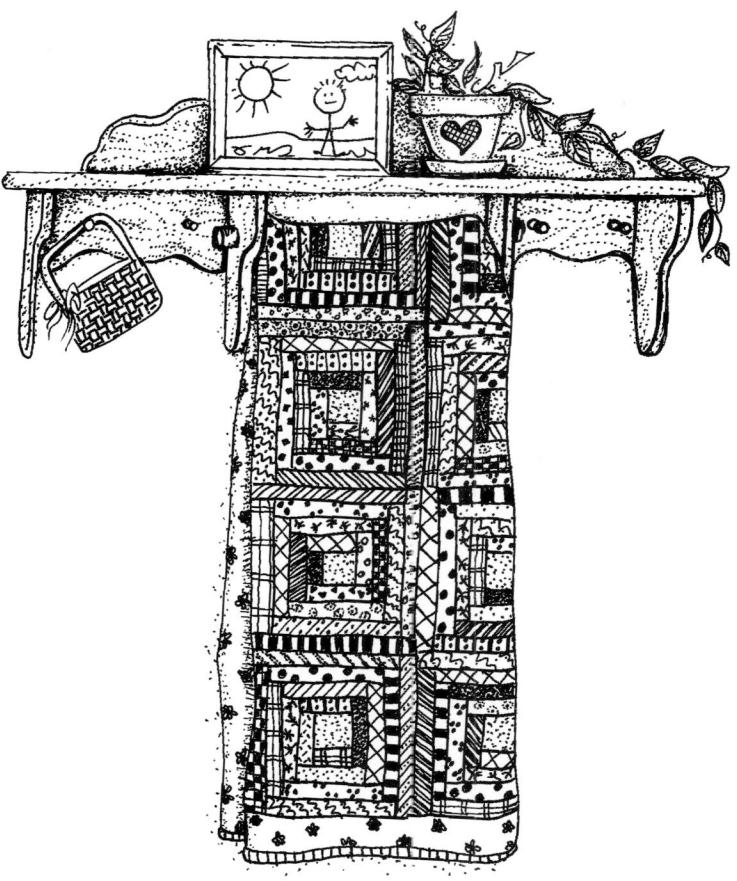

32 **Starlight Topper**
See photo index page 3

Sunny Days Star
Topper

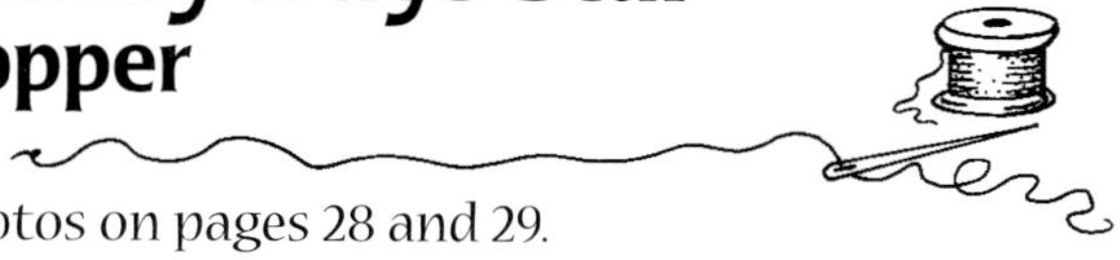

Photos on pages 28 and 29.

Approximate finished size 68x68"

6" block – set 10x10

Use 42-44"-wide fabric. When strips appear in the cutting list, cut crossgrain strips (selvage to selvage).

Yardage

Background – white print	2⅝ yds.
Blocks – light – 4 yellows	⅓ yd. each
dark – 5 blues	½ yd. each
Appliques – hearts – yellow	¼ yd.
Border 1	⅜ yd.
Border 2	⅞ yd.
Backing	4⅜ yds.
Binding	⅝ yd.
Batting	74 x 74"

Cutting Patterns on page 63

Background	for appliques	4 squares – 6½"
	for yellow blocks	16 squares – 7¼"
	for blue blocks	32 squares – 6⅞"
Blocks	yellows	7 strips 1⅜" wide each
	blues	10 strips 1⅜" wide each
Appliques		16
Border 1		7 strips 1½" wide
Border 2		7 strips 3½" wide
Binding		7 strips 2½" wide

Directions

Use ¼" seam allowance unless otherwise noted.

1. Cut 7¼" background squares in **quarters** diagonally. Cut 6⅞" background squares in **half** diagonally.

2. Make 7 strip sets with yellow strips. Press seams in one direction. Using template for yellow strip set on page 63 and diagram at right, cut strip sets into 64 triangles.

3. Make 10 strip sets with blue strips. Press seams in one direction. Using template for blue strip set on page 63 and diagram at right, cut strip sets into 64 triangles.

4. Stitch 2 yellow triangles to 2 white triangles cut from 7¼" background squares as shown. Make 32. Stitch 1 blue triangle to 1 white triangle cut from 6⅞" background squares. Make 64. Press blocks.

5. Applique 4 hearts to each 6½" background square.

6. Stitch blocks into 10 rows of 10, rotating as shown.

7. Stitch rows together. Press.

8. Border 1: Measure length of quilt. Piece border strips to the measured length and stitch to sides of quilt. Repeat at top and bottom. Press.

9. Border 2: Repeat Step 8.

10. Piece backing to same size as batting. Layer and quilt as desired. Trim backing and batting even with top.

11. Stitch binding strips end to end. Press in half lengthwise, wrong sides together. Bind quilt using ⅜" seam allowance.

2. Yellow Strip Sets

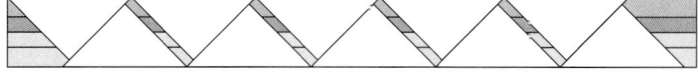

3. Blue Strip Sets

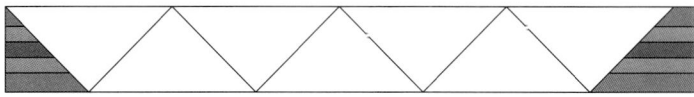

4.

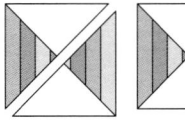

5.

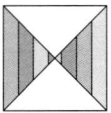

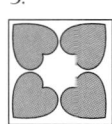

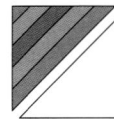

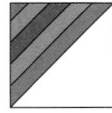

Amish Garden
Topper

Photos on pages 60 and 61.

Approximate finished size 60x60"

6½" block - set 5x5

Use 42-44"-wide fabric. When strips appear in the cutting list, cut crossgrain strips (selvage to selvage).

Yardage

Blocks – dark – black	1¼ yds.
lights – 9-12 brights	¼ yd. each
Appliques – flowers – 9 brights	⅙ yd. each
leaves – 3 greens	⅙ yd. each
vine – green	⅝ yd.
Border 1 – black & white check	⅜ yd.
Border 2 – red	¼ yd.
Border 3 – black	2⅓ yds.
Backing	4 yds.
Binding	⅝ yd.
Batting	66x66"

Cutting Patterns on pages 58 & 69

Blocks	centers (black)	25 squares – 2½"
	logs (black)	25 strips 1¼" wide
	logs (brights)	2-3 strips 1¼" wide each
Appliques		see Step 6b of directions
Border 1		4 strips 1½" wide
Border 2		4 strips 1¼" wide
Border 3		6 strips 12½" wide
Binding		7 strips 2½" wide

Directions

Use ¼" seam allowance unless otherwise noted.

1. Make 25 blocks by stitching strips to center squares in three clockwise rounds. Strips 1 and 2 are light, strips 3 and 4 are dark. After stitching each strip to block, trim off remaining end of strip. See diagram. Press.

   Note: To make all blocks consistent in size, it is best to cut strips for last two rounds to the same length for all blocks. After one round of strips is stitched to all 25 blocks, measure several blocks to get an average length to cut the next strip. Cut 25 strips that length and stitch one to each block. Repeat for remaining 7 strips. All blocks will be exactly the same size and will be much easier to stitch into rows.

2. Stitch blocks into 5 rows of 5, rotating as shown.

3. Stitch rows together. Press.

4. Border 1: Measure length of quilt. Piece border strips to the measured length and stitch to sides of quilt. Repeat at top and bottom. Press.

5. Border 2: Repeat Step 4. Press.

6. Border 3:

   a. Repeat Step 4. Press.

   b. Trace appliques to fusible web: 12 A, 8 B, 8 C, 4 D, 12 E, 16 F, 8 G, 24 H, 38 I, 54 J, 24 vine side segments, 4 vine corner segments, and 4 vine corner segments reversed, using fabrics as desired.

   c. Fuse to desired fabrics and cut out.

   d. Fuse vine segments to one corner quadrant of border as shown in diagram. Repeat for other four corners of quilt.

   e. Fuse flowers and leaves to one corner quadrant of quilt along vine as shown, making sure to cover joins in vine. Cut 8 extra vine side segments into pieces for bluebell and bud stems. Repeat for other four corners of quilt. Stitch in place with machine zigzag or buttonhole stitch.

7. Piece backing to same size as batting. Layer and quilt as desired. Trim backing and batting even with top.

8. Stitch binding strips end to end. Press in half lengthwise, wrong sides together. Bind quilt using ⅜" seam allowance.

1.

Round 1

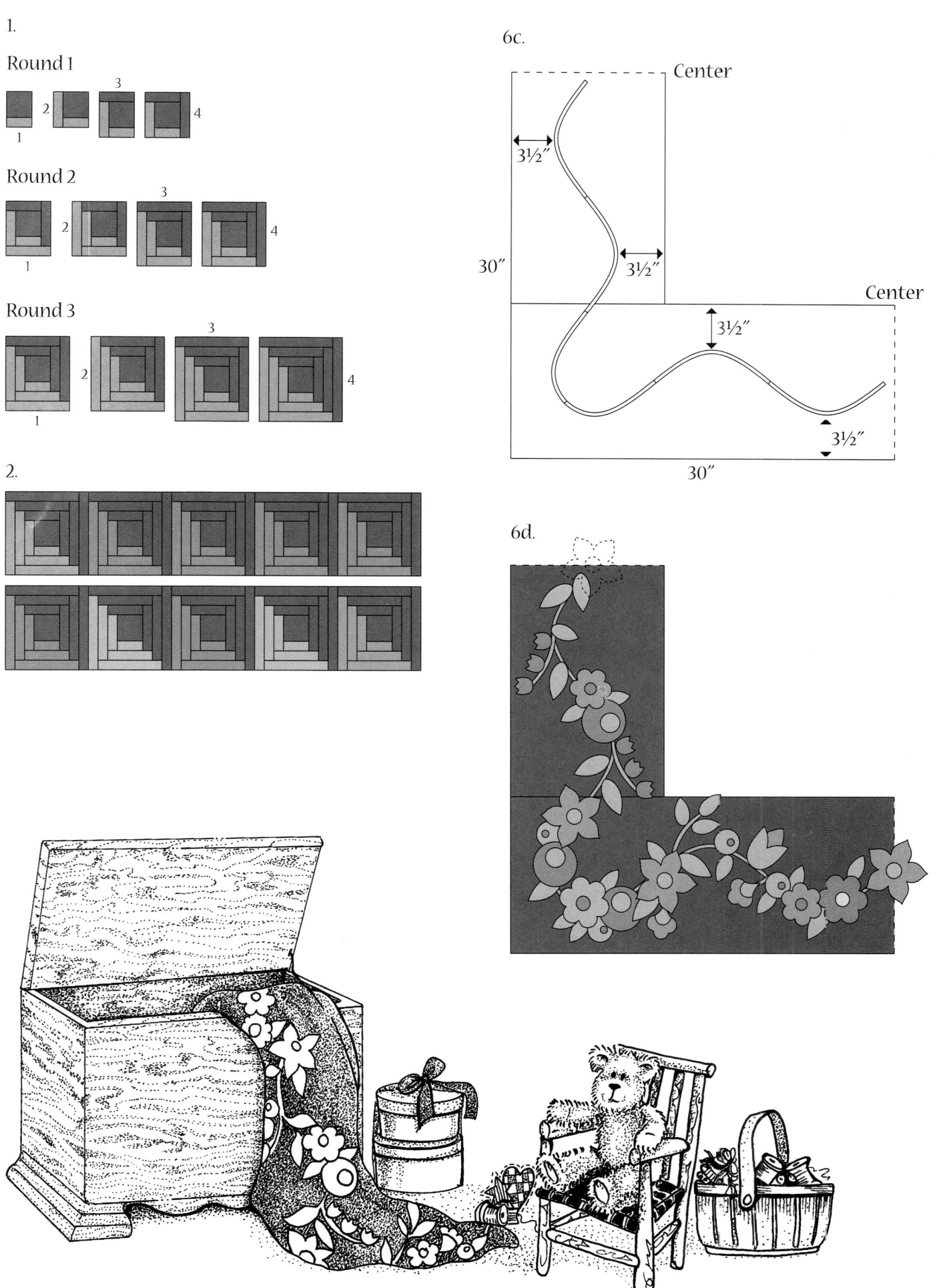

Round 2

Round 3

2.

6c.

Center

3½″

3½″

30″

Center

3½″

3½″

30″

6d.

Amish Garden
Pillow Topper

Double/Queen

Photo on page 61.

Use 42-44"-wide fabric. When strips appear in cutting list, cut crossgrain strips (selvage to selvage).

	Twin	Double/Queen	King
Size Width by height	48x38"	70x38"	86x38"

Yardage

	Twin	Double/Queen	King
Background – black	1½ yds.	2¼ yds.	2⅝ yds.
Flowers – 9 brights	⅙ yd. each	⅙ yd. each	⅙ yd. each
Leaves – 3 greens	⅛ yd. each	⅛ yd. each	⅛ yd. each
Vine – green	¼ yd.	½ yd.	½ yd.
Backing	1½ yds.	2¼ yds.	2⅝ yds.
Binding	½ yd.	½ yd.	⅝ yd.
Batting	52x42"	74x42"	90x42"

Cutting Patterns on pages 58 & 67

	Twin	Double/Queen	King
Background	48x38"	70x38"	86x38"
Appliques	*	**	***
Binding – 2½" strips	5	6	7

* 4 A, 1 B, 1 C, 1 D, 4 E, 3 F, 1 G, 6 H, 12 I, 7 J, & 4 vine segments

** 5 A, 3 B, 2 C, 1 D, 5 E, 6 F, 3 G, 6 H, 15 I, 11 J, & 6 vine segments

*** 6 A, 4 B, 2 C, 1 D, 7 E, 8 F, 4 G, 9 H, 17 I, 14 J, & 9 vine segments

Directions

1. Applique:

   a. Make full-sized vine segment template following directions on page 67. Draw around template on fusible web for vine segments, and trace other appliques directly to fusible web. Fuse to desired fabrics and cut out.

   b. Fuse vine segments to bottom design area of pillow topper, trimming ends where shown. See diagram.

   c. Fuse flowers and leaves along vine, making sure to cover joins in vine. Cut extra vine segments into pieces for bluebell stems. Stitch in place with machine zigzag or buttonhole stitch.

2. Cut backing to same size as batting. Layer and quilt as desired. Trim backing and batting even with top.

3. Stitch binding strips end to end. Press in half lengthwise, wrong sides together. Bind pillow topper using ⅜″ seam allowance.

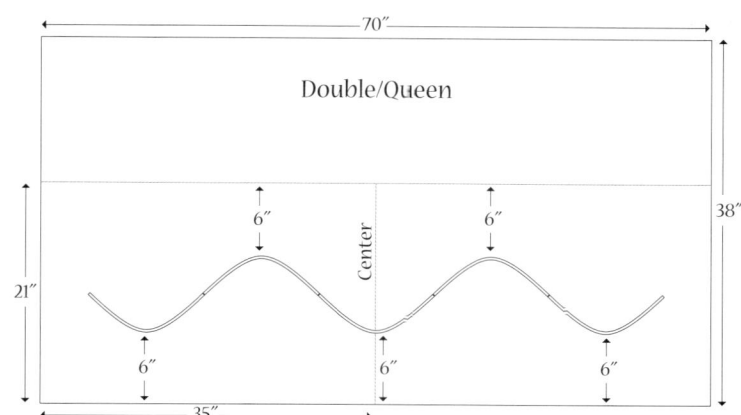

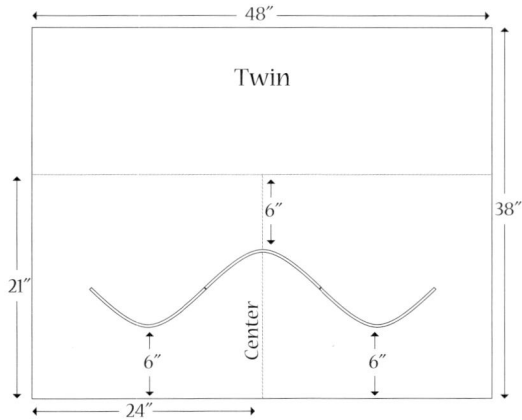

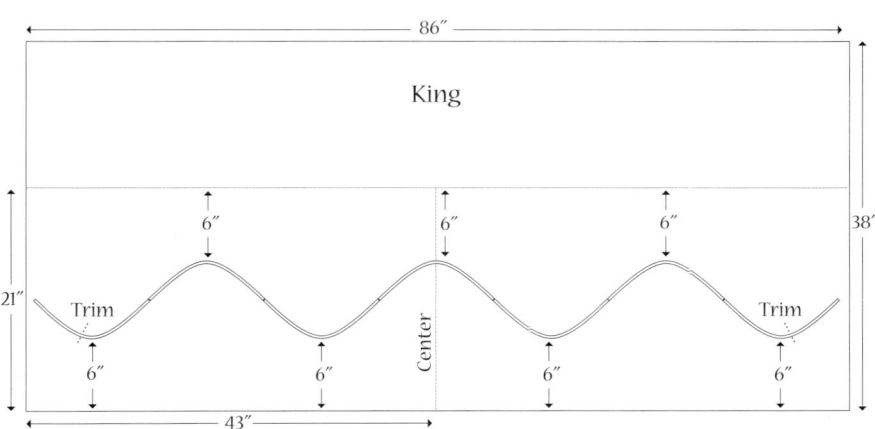

37

Starlight
Topper

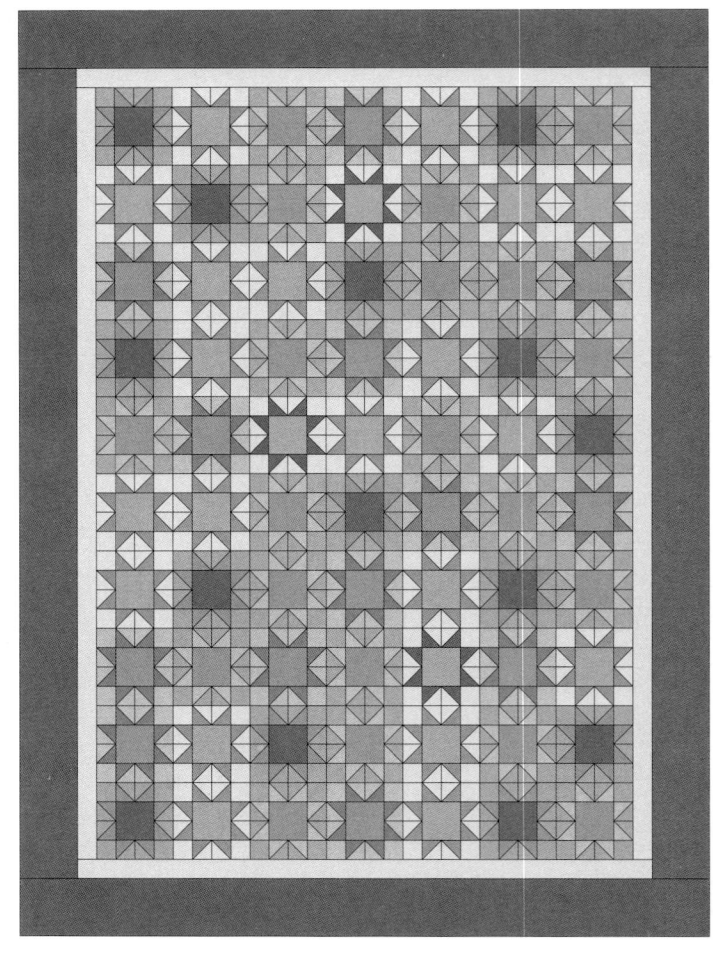

Photo on pages 32 and 53.

Approximate finished size 72 x 96"

8" block – set 7 x 10

Use 42-44"-wide fabric. When strips appear in the cutting list, cut crossgrain strips (selvage to selvage).

Yardage

Blocks – blue batiks to total	6¾ yds.
Border 1	⅝ yd.
Border 2	1¾ yds.
Backing	6 yds.
Binding	¾ yd.
Batting	78 x 102"

Cutting

One block	blue (center)	1 square – 4½"
	blue (star points)	4 squares – 2⅞"
	bkgrnd (sides)	4 squares – 2⅞"
	bkgrnd (corners)	4 squares – 2½"
Border 1		7 strips 2½" wide
Border 2		8 strips 6½" wide
Binding		9 strips 2½" wide

Directions

Use ¼" seam allowance unless otherwise noted.

1. Cut 2⅞" squares in **half** diagonally.

2. Make 70 blocks as shown. Press.

3. Stitch blocks into 10 rows of 7.

4. Stitch rows together. Press.

5. Border 1: Measure length of quilt. Piece border strips to the measured length and stitch to sides of quilt. Repeat at top and bottom. Press.

6. Border 2: Repeat Step 4.

7. Piece backing vertically to same size as batting. Layer and quilt as desired. Trim backing and batting even with top.

8. Stitch binding strips end to end. Press in half lengthwise, wrong sides together. Bind quilt using ⅜" seam allowance.

2. For One Block

   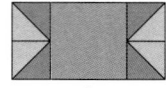

Make 8   Make 4   Make 2   Make 1

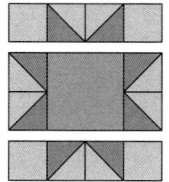 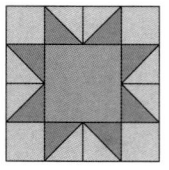

3.

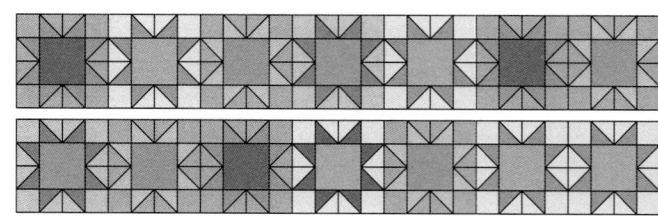

Starlight
Pillow Covers

Photo on page 53. Open end, turned edges.

Use 42-44"-wide fabric. When strips appear in cutting list, cut crossgrain strips (selvage to selvage).

Yardage   Makes 2

	STANDARD	QUEEN	KING
	20x30"	20x34"	20x40"
Main fabric – blue batik	1⅜ yds.	1⅝ yds.	2 yds.
Blocks – 10 blue batiks	⅙ yd. ea.	⅙ yd. ea.	⅙ yd. ea.
Border – light blue batik	⅓ yd.	⅓ yd.	⅓ yd.
Backing for quilting	2¾ yds.	2¾ yds.	2¾ yds.
Binding	⅓ yd.	⅓ yd.	⅓ yd.
Batting – 2 pieces	45x34"	45x38"	45x44"

Cutting

	STANDARD	QUEEN	KING
Main fabric – 2 pieces	21x40½"	25x40½"	31x40½"
Blocks	see Step 1 at right		
Border – 1¼" strips	2-3	2-3	2-3
1½" strips	2-3	2-3	2-3
Binding – 2½" strips	2-3	2-3	2-3

Directions

Use ¼" seam allowance unless otherwise noted.

1. Make 10 blocks following cutting chart and directions on page 38. Stitch into 2 rows of 5 blocks. Stitch 1¼" border strip to one side of each row and 1½" border strip to other side. Stitch large background piece to side with 1¼" strip. Make two. Press.

2. Cut backing to same size as batting. Layer and quilt as desired. Trim backing and batting even with top.

3. Fold in half, right sides together, matching ends of row of blocks and ¾" border. Stitch side and end without patchwork with a ½" seam allowance. Clip corner and turn.

4. Stitch binding strips end to end, if necessary, to make long enough to fit. Press in half lengthwise, wrong sides together. Bind pillow covers using ⅜" seam allowance.

Standard

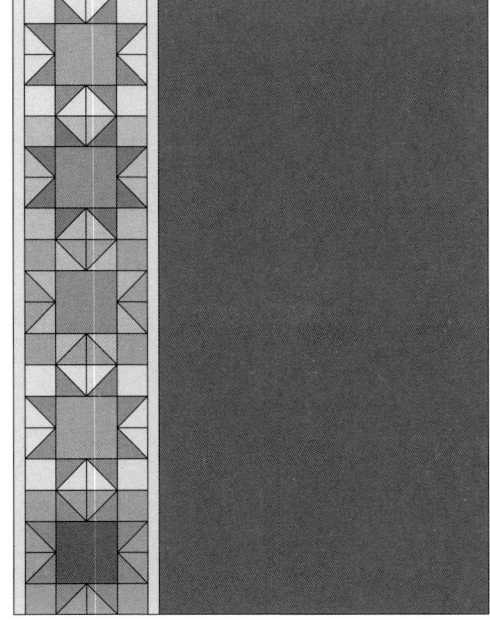

Bind

Paint Box Plaids
Topper

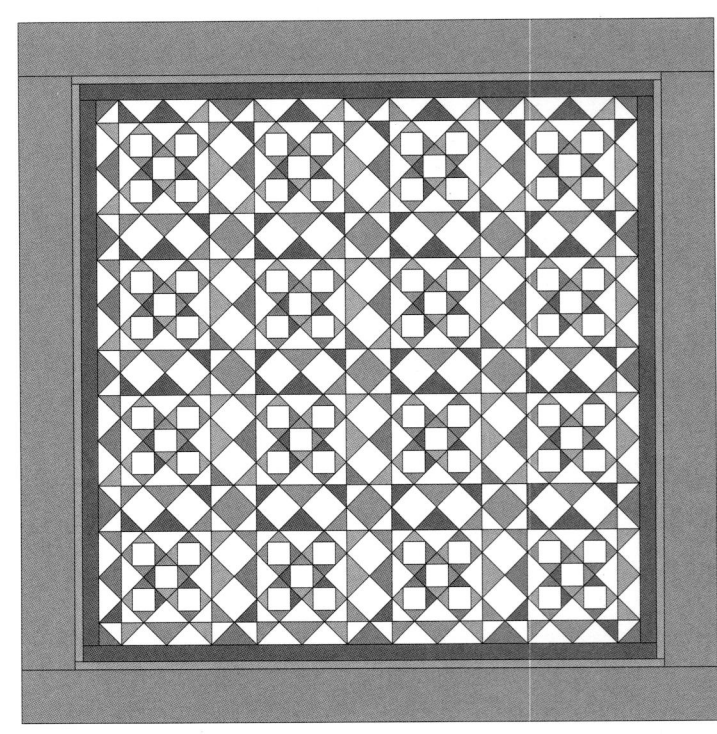

Photo on page 24.

Approximate finished size 65x65"

9" blocks – set diagonally

Use 42-44"-wide fabric. When strips appear in the cutting list, cut crossgrain strips (selvage to selvage).

Yardage

Background – white print	2⅓ yds.
Stars – bright plaids to total	2¾ yds.
Border 1	½ yd.
Border 2	⅓ yd.
Border 3	1⅜ yds.
Backing	4¼ yds.
Binding	⅝ yd.
Batting	71x71"

Cutting

Block 1	bkgrnd	A	80 squares – 2⅝"
		B	32 squares – 3⅞"
	plaids	B	32 squares – 3⅞"
		C	160 squares – 2⅜"
Block 2	bkgrnd	D	36 squares – 3½"
		E	18 squares – 4¼"
	plaids	D	9 squares – 3½"
		E	18 squares – 4¼"
Half-blocks	bkgrnd	B	12 squares – 3⅞"
		D	12 squares – 3½"
		E	12 squares – 4¼"
	plaids	B	6 squares – 3⅞"
		E	12 squares – 4¼"
Qtr-blocks	bkgrnd	B	4 squares – 3⅞"
		E	2 squares – 4¼"
	plaids	E	3 squares – 4¼"
Border 1			6 strips 2" wide
Border 2			6 strips 1¼" wide
Border 3			7 strips 5½" wide
Binding			7 strips 2½" wide

Directions

Use ¼" seam allowance unless otherwise noted.

1. For Block 1, cut 3⅞" squares and 2⅜" squares in **half** diagonally. Make 16 Block 1 as shown. Press.

2. For Block 2, cut 4¼" squares in **quarters** diagonally. Make 9 Block 2 as shown. Make 12 half-blocks and 4 quarter-blocks as shown. Press.

3. Lay out blocks, alternating Block 1 and Block 2, with half-blocks around edge and quarter-blocks in corners. Stitch diagonal rows of blocks, as shown.

4. Stitch rows together. Note: Outside edge is all bias. Staystitch inside ¼" seam allowance if desired. Press.

5. Border 1: Measure length of quilt. Piece border strips to the measured length and stitch to sides of quilt. Repeat at top and bottom. Press.

6. Border 2: Repeat Step 5.

7. Border 3: Repeat Step 5.

8. Piece backing to same size as batting. Layer and quilt as desired. Trim backing and batting even with top.

9. Stitch binding strips end to end. Press in half lengthwise, wrong sides together. Bind quilt using ⅜" seam allowance.

1. Block 1

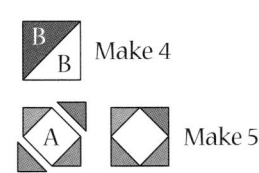

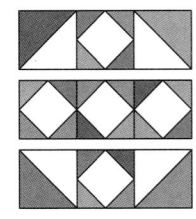

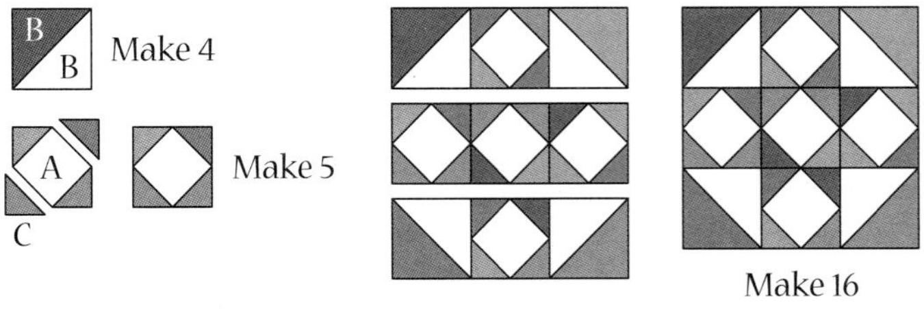

Make 16

2. Block 2

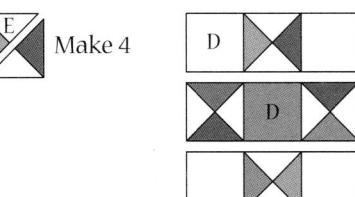

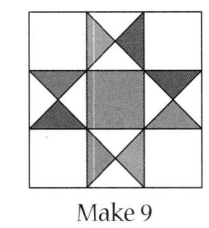

Make 9

Half-Block

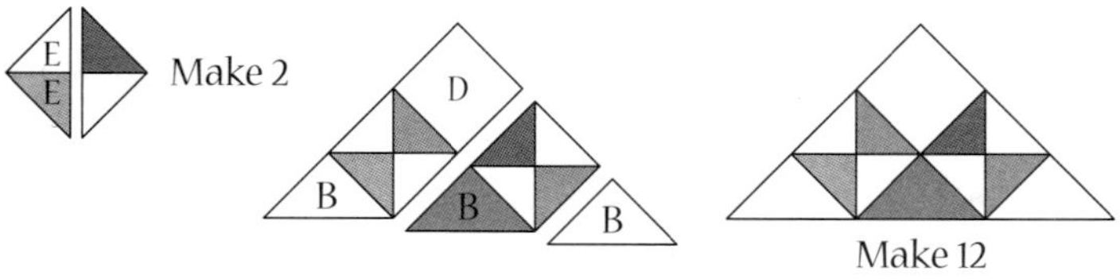

Quarter-Block

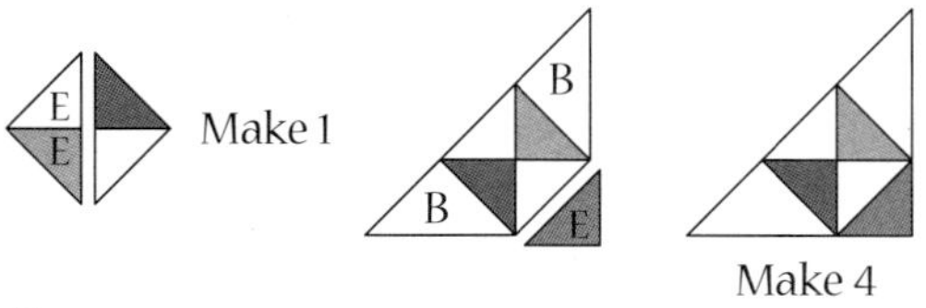

3.

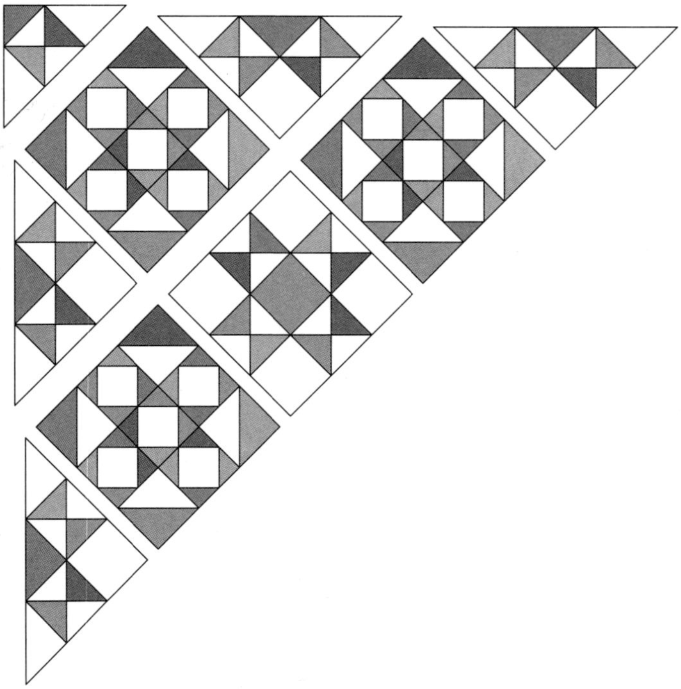

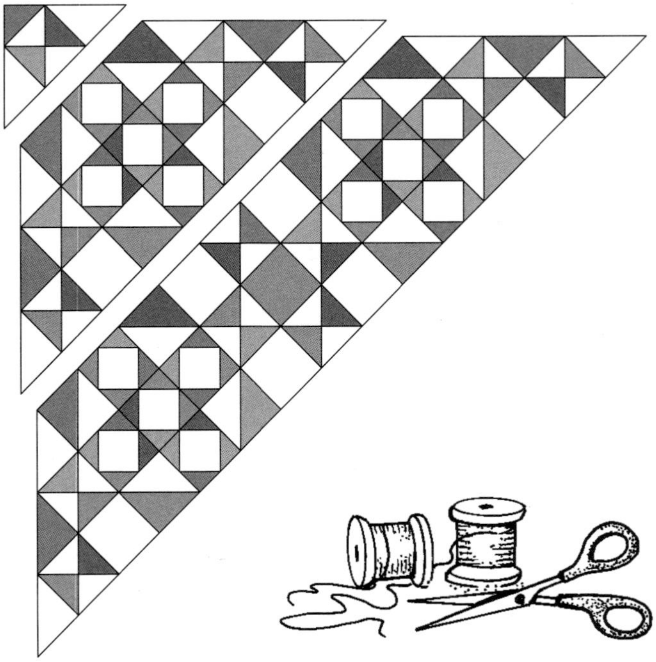

Paint Box Plaids

Throw Pillow

Photo on page 24.

Use 42-44″-wide fabric. When strips appear in the cutting list, cut crossgrain strips (selvage to selvage).

Yardage Makes one 18″ pillow

Background – white print	1/6 yd.
Star – bright plaid	1/6 yd.
Borders 1-3	1/4 yd. each
Backing for quilting	3/4 yd.
Backing for pillow	3/4 yd.
Binding	1/4 yd.
Batting	22 x 22″
18″ pillow form	

Cutting

Block	bkgrnd	D	4 squares – 3½″
		E	2 squares – 4¼″
	plaids	D	1 square – 3½″
		E	2 squares – 4¼″
Borders 1-3			2 strips 2″ wide each fabric
Backing for pillow			2 pieces 18½ x 22″
Binding			2 strips 2½″ wide

Directions

1. Make one Block 2 using diagrams and directions on page 40.
2. Stitch 2″ strips to two opposite sides of block, then two remaining sides. After stitching each strip to block, trim off remaining end of strip. Attach remaining strips in same manner. Press.
3. Cut backing for quilting the same size as batting. Layer and quilt as desired. Trim backing and batting even with top.
4. Press 18½ x 22″ pieces for envelope back in half, wrong sides together, to 18½ x 11″. Place both pieces on wrong side of pillow top, matching raw edges and overlapping folded edges in center. Baste outside edge.
5. Stitch binding strips end to end. Press in half lengthwise, wrong sides together. Bind using 3/8″ seam allowance. Insert pillow form.

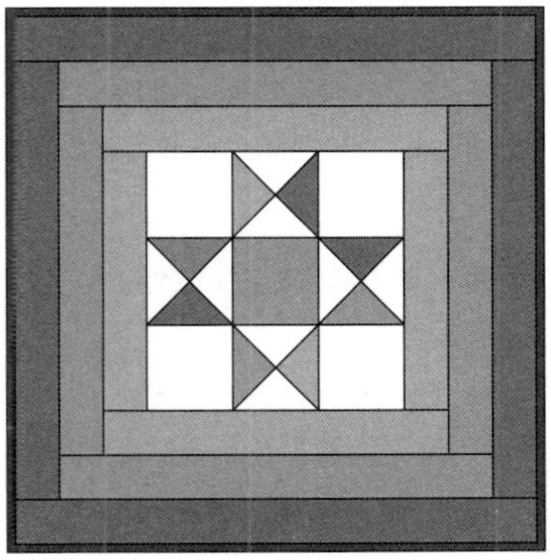

Lazy Daisy
Topper

Photos on page 64 and back cover.

Approximate finished size 60x60"

20" blocks – set 3x3

Use 42-44"-wide fabric. When strips appear in the cutting list, cut crossgrain strips (selvage to selvage).

Yardage

Block centers – white print	½ yd.
Logs – pastel prints to total	5½ yds.
Appliques – flower – white	¼ yd.
flower center – gold	⅛ yd.
stem & leaves – green	⅙ yd.
Backing	4 yds.
Binding	⅝ yd.
Batting	66x66"

Cutting   Patterns on page 59

Block centers	9 squares – 6½"
Logs	110-120 strips – 1½" wide
Appliques	9 each
Binding	7 strips 2½" wide

Directions

Use ¼" seam allowance unless otherwise noted.

1. Make 9 blocks by stitching strips to center squares, two opposite sides first, then two remaining opposite sides. After stitching each strip to block, trim off remaining end of strip. See diagram. Press.

   Note: To make all blocks consistent in size, it is best to cut strips for the last three rounds to the same length for all blocks before sewing. After fourth round of strips is stitched to all 9 blocks, measure several blocks to get an average length to cut the next strip. Cut 18 strips that length and stitch to opposite sides of each block. Repeat for remaining strips. All blocks will be exactly the same size and will be much easier to stitch into rows.

2. Applique flowers to centers of blocks, overlapping first row of strips in various ways.

3. Stitch blocks into 3 rows of 3, rotating as desired.

4. Stitch rows together. Press.

5. Piece backing to same size as batting. Layer and quilt as desired. Trim backing and batting even with top.

6. Stitch binding strips end to end. Press in half lengthwise, wrong sides together. Bind quilt using ⅜" seam allowance.

1.

Round 1   Round 2

Round 3

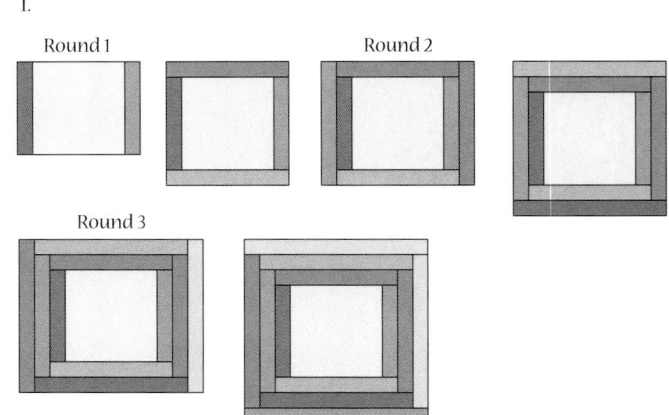

2.

Lazy Daisy
Throw Pillows

Photo on page 64.

Use 42-44"-wide fabric. When strips appear in the cutting list, cut crossgrain strips (selvage to selvage).

Yardage   Makes one 20" pillow

Block center – white print	¼ yd.
Logs – 7 pastel prints	⅙ yd. each
Appliques – flower – white	⅙ yd.
flower center – gold	⅛ yd.
stem & leaves – green	⅛ yd.
Backing for quilting	¾ yd.
Backing for pillow	⅞ yd.
Binding	⅓ yd.
Batting	24 x 24"
20" pillow form	

Cutting   Patterns on page 59

Block center	1 square – 6½"
Logs	1-3 strips each fabric – 1½" wide
Applique	1 each
Backing for pillow	2 pieces 20½ x 28"
Binding	2-3 strips 2½" wide

Directions

1. Make 1 block using diagrams and directions on page 42.

2. Cut backing for quilting the same size as batting. Layer and quilt as desired. Trim backing and batting even with top.

3. Press 20½ x 28" pieces for envelope back in half, wrong sides together to 20½ x 14". Place both pieces on wrong side of pillow top, matching raw edges and overlapping folded edges in center. Baste outside edge.

4. Stitch binding strips end to end. Press in half lengthwise, wrong sides together. Bind using ⅜" seam allowance. Insert pillow form.

Patch of Blue
Topper

Photo on page 57.

Approximate finished size 70x78"

6¼" blocks – set diagonally 7x8

Use 42-44"-wide fabric. When strips appear in the cutting list, cut crossgrain strips (selvage to selvage).

Yardage

Background – blocks & border – white	5¼ yds.
Blocks – 4 shades of blue	⅝ yd. each
Backing	5 yds.
Binding	⅔ yd.
Batting	76x84"

Cutting

Background	blocks	31 strips 1¾" wide
	setting squares	42 squares – 6¾"
	side triangles	7 squares – 10⅛"
	corner triangles	2 squares – 5¼"
	border	8 strips 4½" wide
Blues	blocks	34 strips 1¾" wide
Binding		8 strips 2½" wide

Directions

Use ¼" seam allowance unless otherwise noted.

1. Blocks:

    a. Make 8 of Strip Set 1 and 5 of Strip Set 2, as shown, mixing blues in strip sets as desired.

    b. Press seam allowances all one way in each set.

    c. Square up the end of each set and then crosscut into 1¾" segments.

    d. Stitch blocks as shown, alternating seam allowance directions for each seam.

    e. Press blocks with seam allowances all going one way.

2. Cut 10⅛" squares in **quarters** diagonally. Cut 5¼" squares in **half** diagonally.

3. Lay out blocks and setting squares and triangles. Stitch diagonal rows of blocks, as shown.

4. Stitch rows together. Press.

5. Border: Measure length of quilt. Piece border strips to the measured length and stitch to sides of quilt. Repeat at top and bottom. Press.

6. Piece backing vertically to same size as batting. Layer and quilt as desired. Trim backing and batting even with top.

7. Stitch binding strips end to end. Press in half lengthwise, wrong sides together. Bind quilt using ⅜" seam allowance.

1.

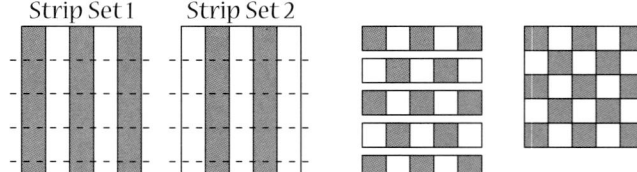

Strip Set 1   Strip Set 2

3.

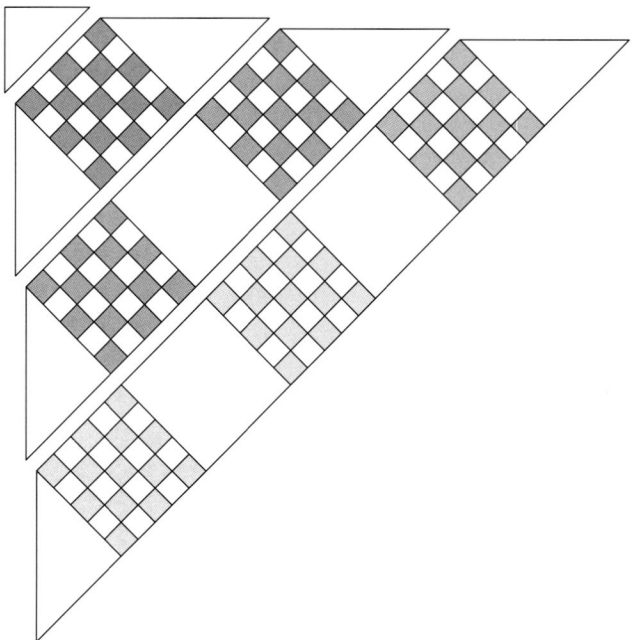

Patch of Blue
Pillow Covers

Photo on page 57. Open end, turned edges.

Use 42-44"-wide fabric. When strips appear in cutting list, cut crossgrain strips (selvage to selvage).

Yardage Makes 2

	STANDARD	QUEEN	KING
	20x30"	20x34"	20x40"
Main fabric, flower centers – blue print	1½ yds.	1⅝ yds.	2 yds.
Applique background – blue	⅓ yd.	⅓ yd.	⅓ yd.
Flowers, leaves, vine – white	⅜ yd.	⅜ yd.	⅜ yd.
Border & binding – white	½ yd.	½ yd.	½ yd.
Backing for quilting	2¾ yds.	2¾ yds.	2¾ yds.
Batting – 2 pieces	45x34"	45x38"	45x44"

Cutting Patterns on pages 62-63

	STANDARD	QUEEN	KING
Main fabric – 2 pieces	22x42"	26x42"	32x42"
Applique background	8½x42"	8½x42"	8½x42"
Border – 1" strips	2-3	2-3	2-3
Appliques – flower centers	10	10	10
flowers	10	10	10
leaves	12	12	12
vine segment	14	14	14
Binding – 3" strips	2-3	2-3	2-3

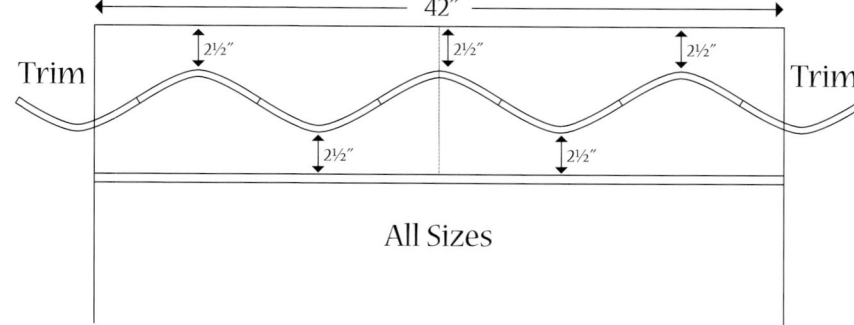

Trim — 42" — Trim

2½" 2½" 2½"

2½" 2½"

All Sizes

Directions

Use ¼" seam allowance unless otherwise noted.

1. Stitch 8½" rectangle to 1" strip, then stitch 21" rectangle to side with 1" strip. Press.

2. Applique

   a. Trace appliques to fusible web. Use the two leaf patterns as desired. We reversed some for variety. Fuse to desired fabrics and cut out.

   b. Fuse vine segments to center panel of pillow topper, trimming ends where shown.

   c. Fuse flowers and leaves along vine, making sure to cover joins in vine. Machine zigzag or buttonhole stitch.

3. Cut backing to same size as batting. Layer and quilt as desired. Trim backing and batting even with top.

4. Fold in half, right sides together, matching ends of row of applique and 1" border. Stitch side and end without applique with a ½" seam allowance. Clip corner and turn.

5. Stitch binding strips end to end, if necessary, to make long enough to fit. Press in half lengthwise, wrong sides together. Bind pillow covers using ½" seam allowance.

Patch of Blue
Appliqued Overlap Comforter Cover

Photo on page 57.

This comforter cover has an appliqued and quilted overlap. Use yardage chart on page 6 for Overlap Comforter Cover, contrasting front and front overlap. Use directions on page 8 for cutting and piecing front and front overlap, except cut overlap 24″ deep instead of 29″. Continue with directions below for appliqued and quilted overlap. Do not hem front overlap.

Use 42-44″-wide fabric. When strips appear in the cutting list, cut crossgrain strips (selvage to selvage).

Yardage

TWIN

Appliques	flowers, leaves, vine, binding – white	1 yd.
	flower centers – blue print	⅛ yd.
Backing for quilted overlap		2 yds.
Batting		28x69″

DOUBLE/QUEEN

Appliques	flowers, leaves, vine, binding – white	1¼ yds.
	flower centers – blue print	⅛ yd.
Backing for quilted overlap		2⅝ yds.
Batting		28x91″

KING

Appliques	flowers, leaves, vine, binding – white	1⅜ yds.
	flower centers – blue print	⅛ yd.
Backing for quilted overlap		3⅛ yds.
Batting		28x107″

Cutting   Patterns on pages 62 & 70

TWIN

Appliques	11 flowers, 12 leaves, 5 vine segments
Binding	2 strips 2½″ wide

DOUBLE/QUEEN

Appliques	15 flowers, 16 leaves, 7 vine segments
Binding	3 strips 2½″ wide

KING

Appliques	19 flowers, 16 leaves, 9 vine segments
Binding	3 strips 2½″ wide

Directions

1. Applique:

   a. Make full-sized vine segment template following directions on page 70. Draw around template on fusible web for vine segments, and trace other appliques directly to fusible web. Fuse to fabrics and cut out.

   b. Fuse vine segments to overlap rectangle, trimming ends where shown. See diagram.

   c. Fuse flowers and leaves along vine, making sure to cover joins in vine. Stitch in place with machine zigzag or buttonhole stitch.

2. Cut backing to same size as batting. Layer and quilt as desired. Trim backing and batting even with top.

3. Stitch binding strips end to end. Press in half lengthwise, wrong sides together. Bind bottom edge of overlap using ⅜″ seam allowance.

4. Continue with directions for assembling comforter cover on page 8.

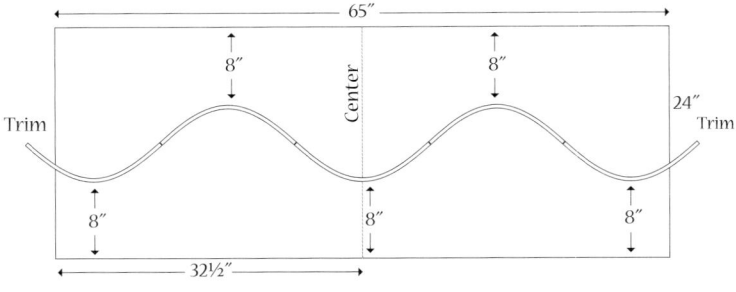

Twin

46

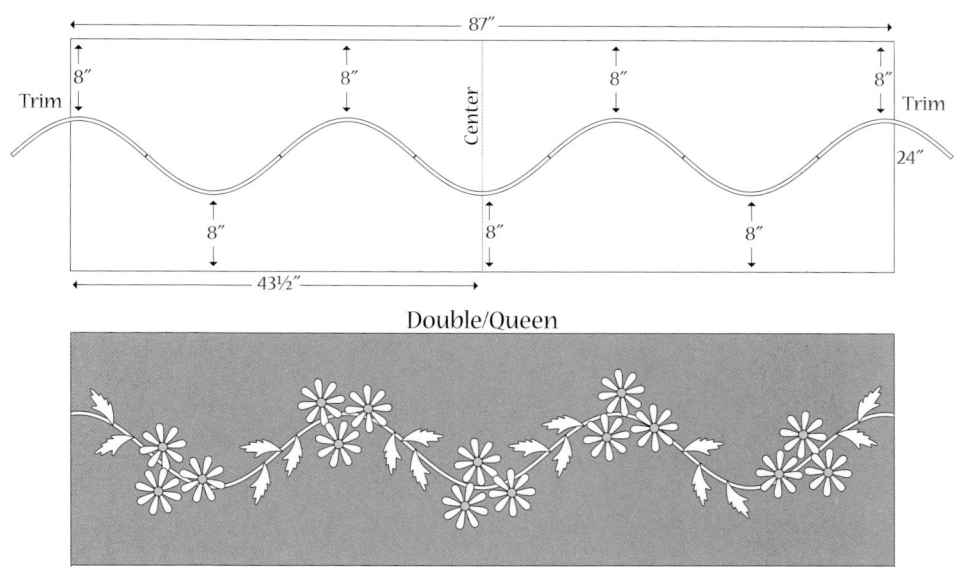

Double/Queen

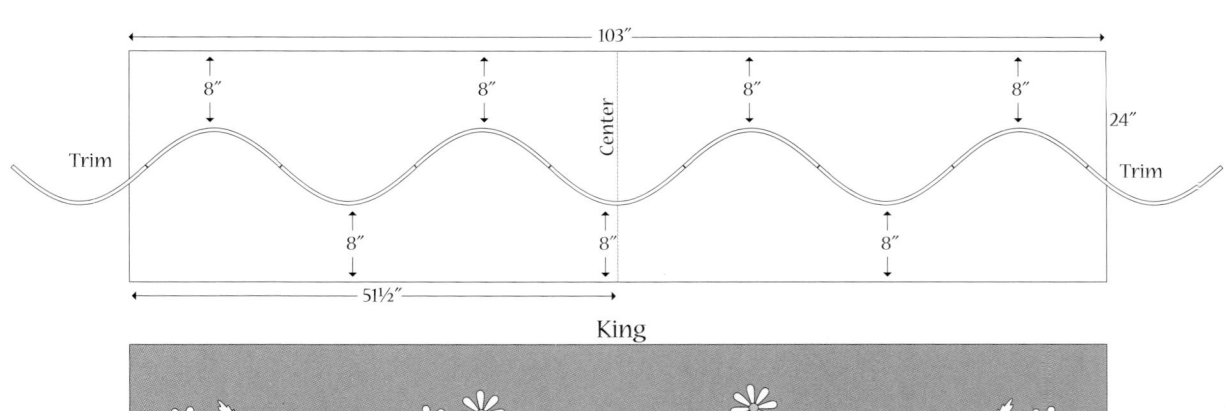

King

Pillowcases

Photos on pages 20, 25, 28, 52, and 56.

Use 42-44"-wide fabric.

Yardage   Makes 2

	STANDARD	QUEEN	KING
	20x30"	20x34"	20x40"
Fabric	2¼ yds.	2½ yds.	2¾ yds.

Cutting

	STANDARD	QUEEN	KING
Fabric – 2 pieces	41x35"	41x39"	41x45"

Directions

1. Fold pieces in half, right sides together, to: 20½x35" for standard, 20½x39" for queen, 20½x45" for king.

2. Stitch side and one end. Turn right side out.

3. On open end, press ½" to wrong side, then press 4" to wrong side, forming hem. Stitch close to fold. Press.

Doggie Bed Cover

Photo on page 49. **Use 54"-wide fabric.**

Yardage

Purchased dog bed	45" diameter
Front & back	2¾ yds. (**54" wide**)
Appliques – 6 dogs	¼-⅓ yd. each
other pieces	scraps
Snap tape	30"

Cutting   Patterns on pages 65-70

Front & back	2 squares 47"
Bias strip for opening	1x30"
Appliques	1 of each dog
	5 hydrants
	1 set lettering

Directions

1. Fold square for front in quarters as shown. Place pin in corner (center of square) and tie a string to it. Holding string at 23½" from pin, drag it in an arc from corner to corner, marking arc with pencil or pins as you go. Cut along marked line. Open out and lay on back square to cut a matching back.

2. Trace appliques to fusible web. Trace dog bodies in one or two pieces and draw or transfer leg or face lines. Fuse to fabrics and cut out. Press dog appliques to front, 3-4" from edge, evenly spaced from each other. Press hydrants and lettering between dogs. See photo. Stitch drawn leg and face lines with machine zigzag or buttonhole stitch. Stitch outside edges of appliques .

3. Place front and back right sides together. Stitch around outside using a 1" seam allowance, leaving a 30" opening. Turn right side out.

4. At opening, press the 1" seam allowance on the **front** edge to the inside. Pull apart snap tape. Stitch one side of snap tape to **inside** of dog bed front.

5. Stitch bias strip to seam allowance of dog bed back at opening, right sides together, using a ¼" seam allowance. Press bias strip to inside along seam-line, creating a facing. Stitch other side of snap tape to **outside** of dog bed bottom on faced seam allowance, making sure snaps line up with snaps on front.

1.

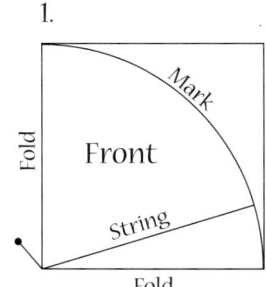

Doggie Place Mat

Photo on page 49. Finished size 14x18"

Use 42-44"-wide fabric.

Yardage

Main fabric	½ yd.
Appliques – dog	¼ yd.
table	¼ yd.
dish	⅛ yd. or scrap
lettering	⅛ yd. or scraps
others	scraps
needlepunch or cotton batting	1 rectangle 14½x18½"

Cutting   Patterns on page 71

Front & back	2 rectangles 14½x18½"
Appliques – table	1 rectangle 6x13"
others	1 each

Directions

Use ¼" seam allowance unless otherwise noted.

1. Applique

   a. Trace appliques to fusible web. Trace dog in one piece. Fuse to fabrics and cut out. Draw or transfer face, leg, and ear lines to dog. Cut off left side of table piece at an angle as shown.

   b. Fuse appliques to place mat front using pattern page and photo as guides.

   c. Stitch drawn face, leg, and ear lines with machine zigzag or buttonhole stitch. Stitch outside edges of appliques .

2. Layer on table:

   batting
   place mat front, right side up
   place mat back, right side down

3. Stitch around place mat, leaving an opening for turning. Turn right side out. Press. Topstitch close to edge and ¼" away.

4. Machine quilt around appliques.

1a.   ←3"→

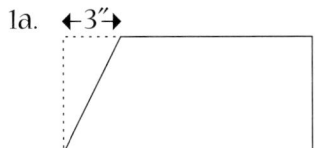

Doggie Bed Cover with our Wonder Dog Ralph, Doggie Place Mat with the lovely dog, Miss Daisy   49

See photo index page 3

Dust Ruffles

Photo on page 56.

Directions are for a ruffle attached with snap tape to a fitted sheet. There is no split at corners for a footboard. The king ruffle is made to fit two extra-long twin fitted sheets to make it easier to change the bed and clean under it. Length of ruffle is 15½". Adjust as needed for different box springs height.

Use 42-44"-wide fabric. When strips appear in cutting list, cut crossgrain strips (selvage to selvage).

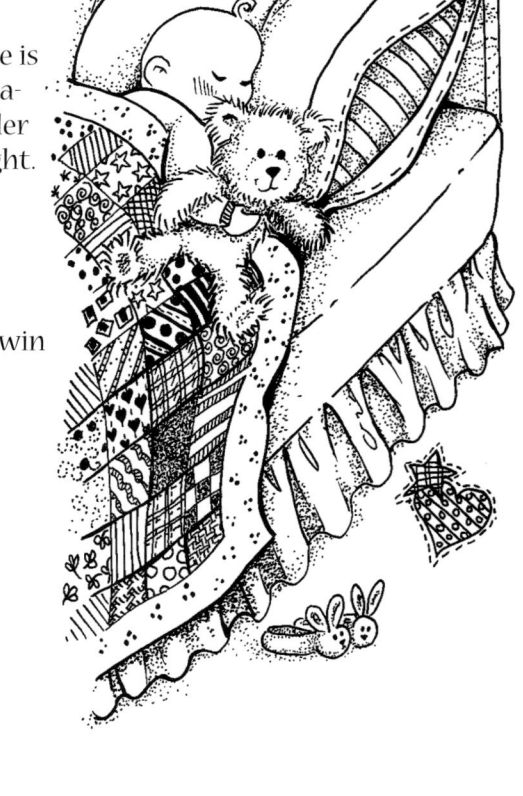

Yardage

	TWIN	X-LONG TWIN	DOUBLE	QUEEN	KING
Fitted sheet(s)	1	1	1	1	2 x-long twin
Ruffle fabric	4⅞ yds.	4⅞ yds.	5⅜ yds.	6 yds.	6½ yds.
Snap tape 1" wide	5⅜ yds.	5⅝ yds.	5¾ yds.	6¼ yds.	7⅛ yds.

Cutting

	TWIN	X-LONG TWIN	DOUBLE	QUEEN	KING
Fabric 18½" strips	9	9	10	11	12

Directions

Use ½" seam allowance unless otherwise noted.

1. Stitch fabric strips together end to end. For king, stitch two sets of 6 strips together.

2. Hem ends: On each end, press ½" to wrong side then press ½" to wrong side again. Stitch close to fold.

3. Hem bottom: On one long edge, press ½" to wrong side then press 2" to wrong side again. Stitch close to fold. Press.

4. Gather: Zigzag over string, crochet cotton, or dental floss ½" from raw edge. Leave long tails of string and backstitch the zigzag at the beginning and end of the stitching line.

5. Put fitted sheet on box springs, adjusting corners as well as possible. Mark top edge of box springs on sheet. For king, mark up second side only about 6-8". You will be making mirror-image ruffles. See diagram. Remove sheet.

6. Separate snap tape. Line up top edge of one half of snap tape along drawn line, and pin in place. Stitch both sides of snap tape. Note: For king, start at head of bed and stitch toward foot of bed. Tape should extend up second side about 6-8". See diagram.

7. Pull up gathers on skirt to fit bed:
   Twin – 189"   Extra-long Twin – 199"   Double – 204"
   Queen – 220"   King – 126" each

8. Pin other half of snap tape to top edge of ruffle on the right side, overlapping raw edge approximately ½", covering zigzag stitching. Stitch in place, straightening folds in ruffle as you stitch. See diagram.

9. Fold snap tape to wrong side and pin in place. Stitch other edge of snap tape to ruffle, straightening folds in ruffle as you stitch.

5-6.

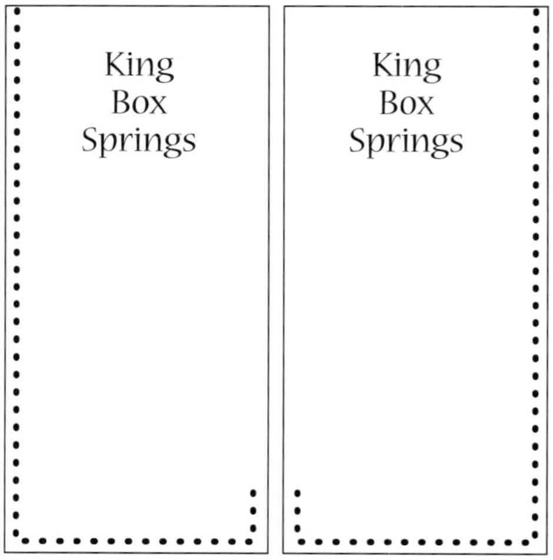

King Box Springs	King Box Springs

8.

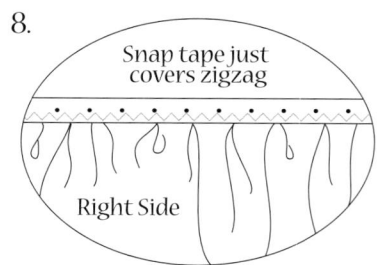

Snap tape just covers zigzag

Right Side

Garden Path
Pillow Covers

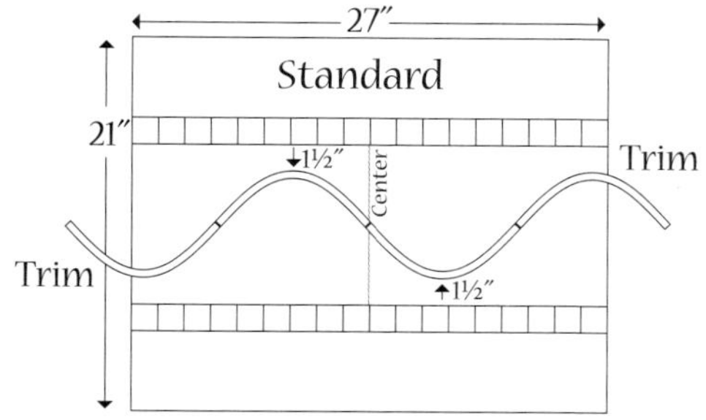

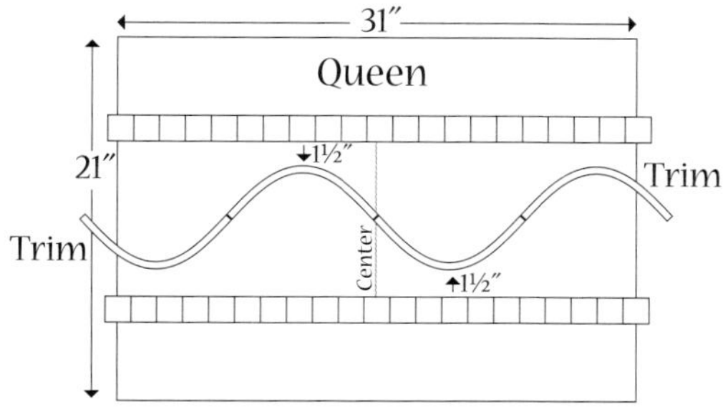

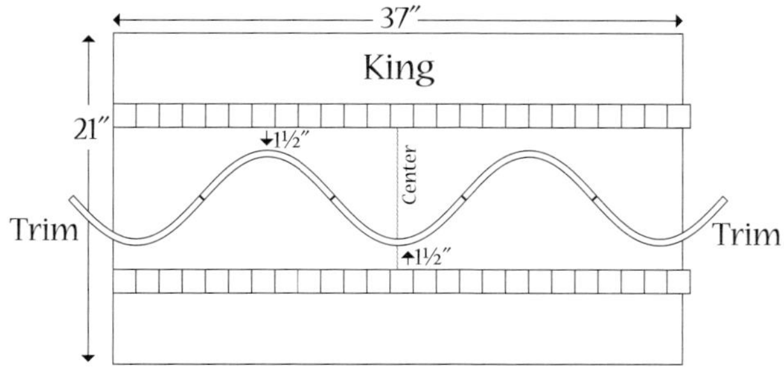

Standard

27″

21″

1½″

Center

Trim

1½″

Trim

Queen

31″

21″

1½″

Center

Trim

1½″

Trim

King

37″

21″

1½″

Center

Trim

1½″

Trim

Twinkle Twinkle
Throw Pillow

Baby design on page 55

Garden Path Quilted Comforter Cover, Pillow Covers, and Pillowcases
See photo index page 3

Twinkle Twinkle
Throw Pillows

54

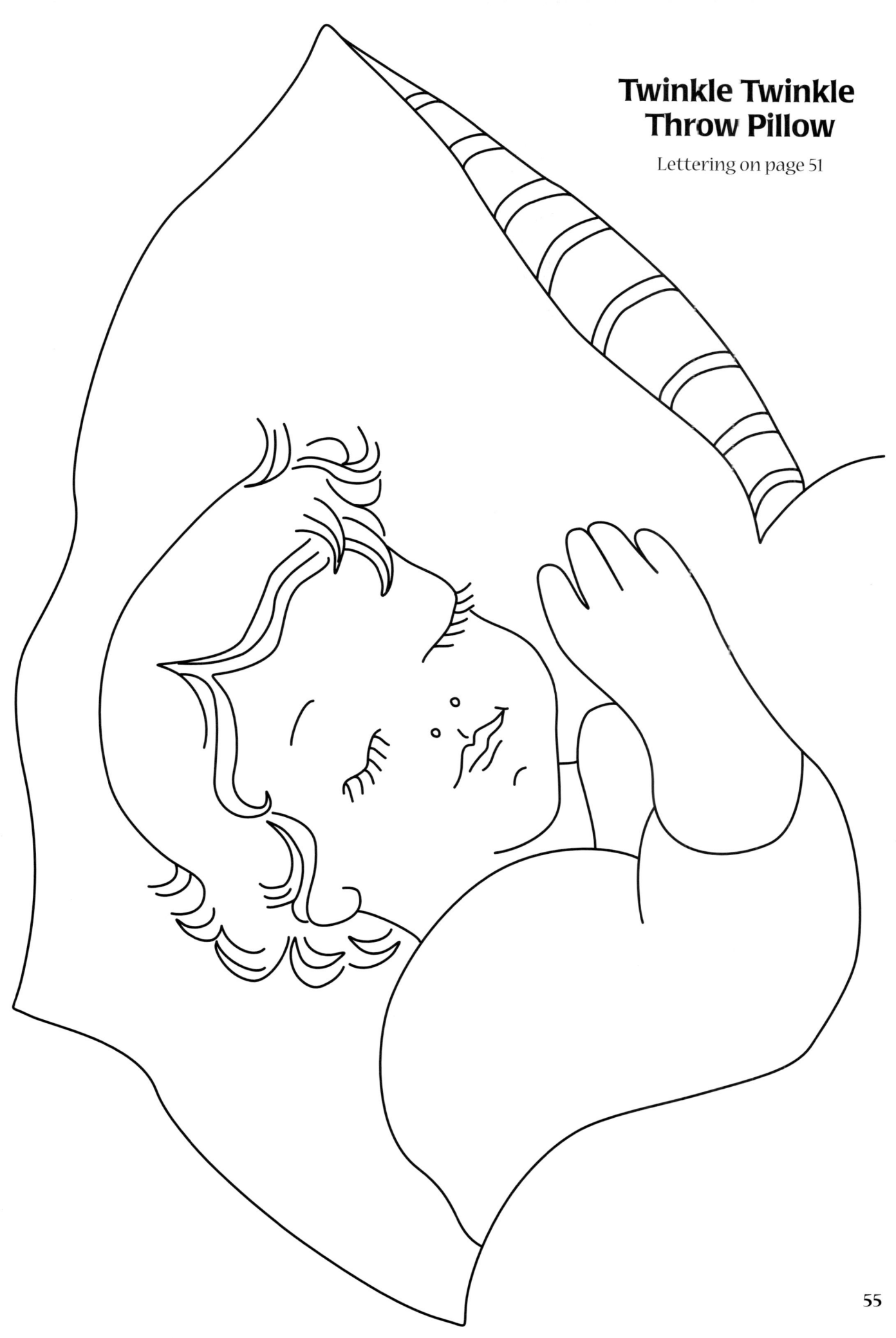

Twinkle Twinkle Quilted Comforter Cover, Throw Pillows, Pillowcases, and Dust Ruffle
See photo index page 3

Patch of Blue Overlap Comforter Cover, Patch of Blue Topper, and Pillow Covers 57

See photo index page 3

Amish Garden Topper & Pillow Topper

Lazy Daisy Topper

Patterns are reversed for tracing to fusible web.

Country Traditions Topper & Throw Pillows

Amish Garden Topper and Amish Garden Pillow Topper   **61**

See photo index page 3

Patch of Blue

Patch of Blue

**Patch of Blue
Comforter Cover
& Pillow Covers**

Patch of Blue

Patterns are reversed for
tracing to fusible web.

Garden Path

**Garden Path
Comforter Cover**

Garden Path

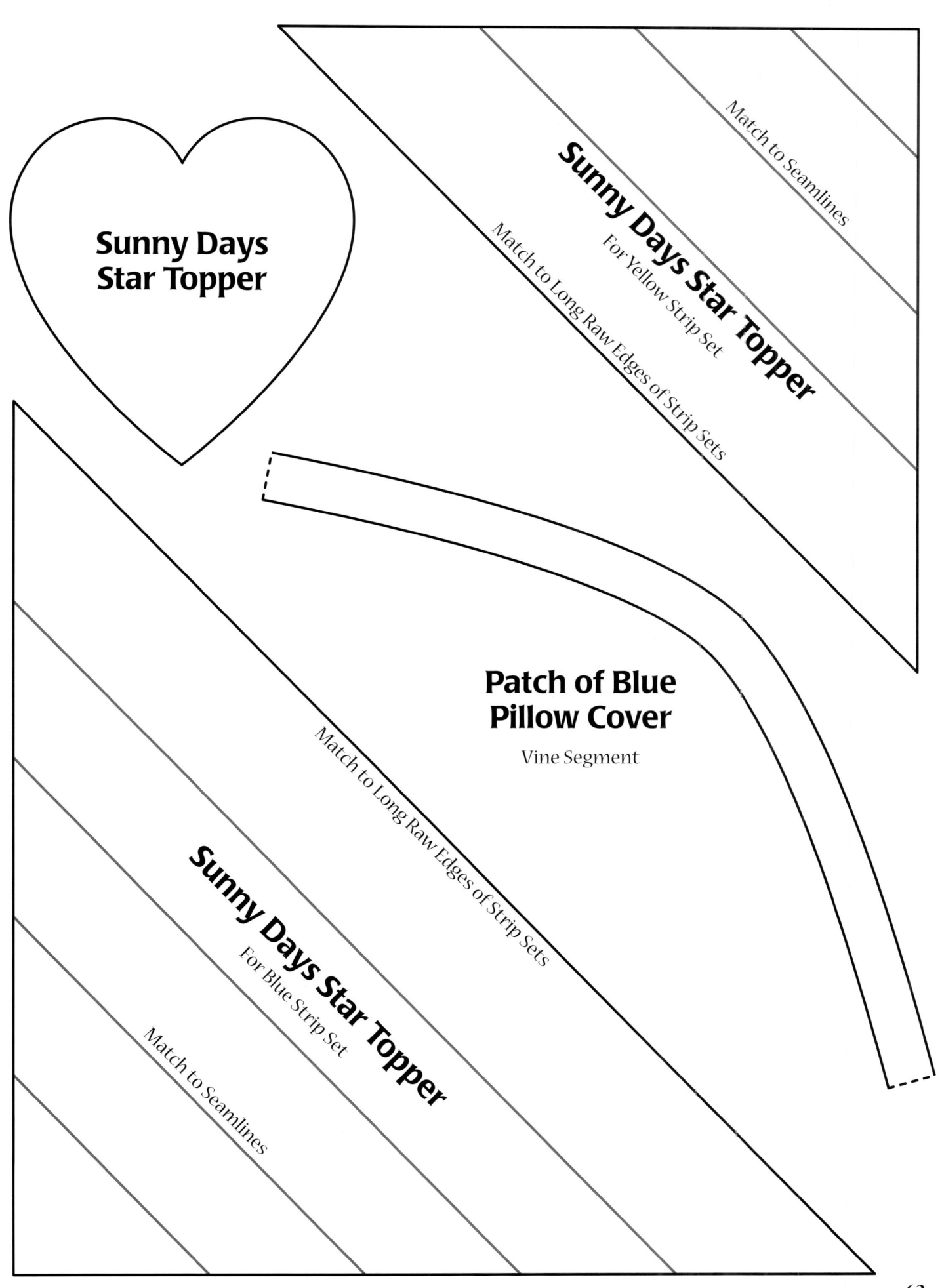

**Sunny Days
Star Topper**

Sunny Days Star Topper

For Yellow Strip Set

Match to Long Raw Edges of Strip Sets

Match to Seamlines

**Patch of Blue
Pillow Cover**

Vine Segment

Match to Long Raw Edges of Strip Sets

Sunny Days Star Topper

For Blue Strip Set

Match to Seamlines

64   Lazy Daisy Topper and Throw Pillows
See photo index page 3

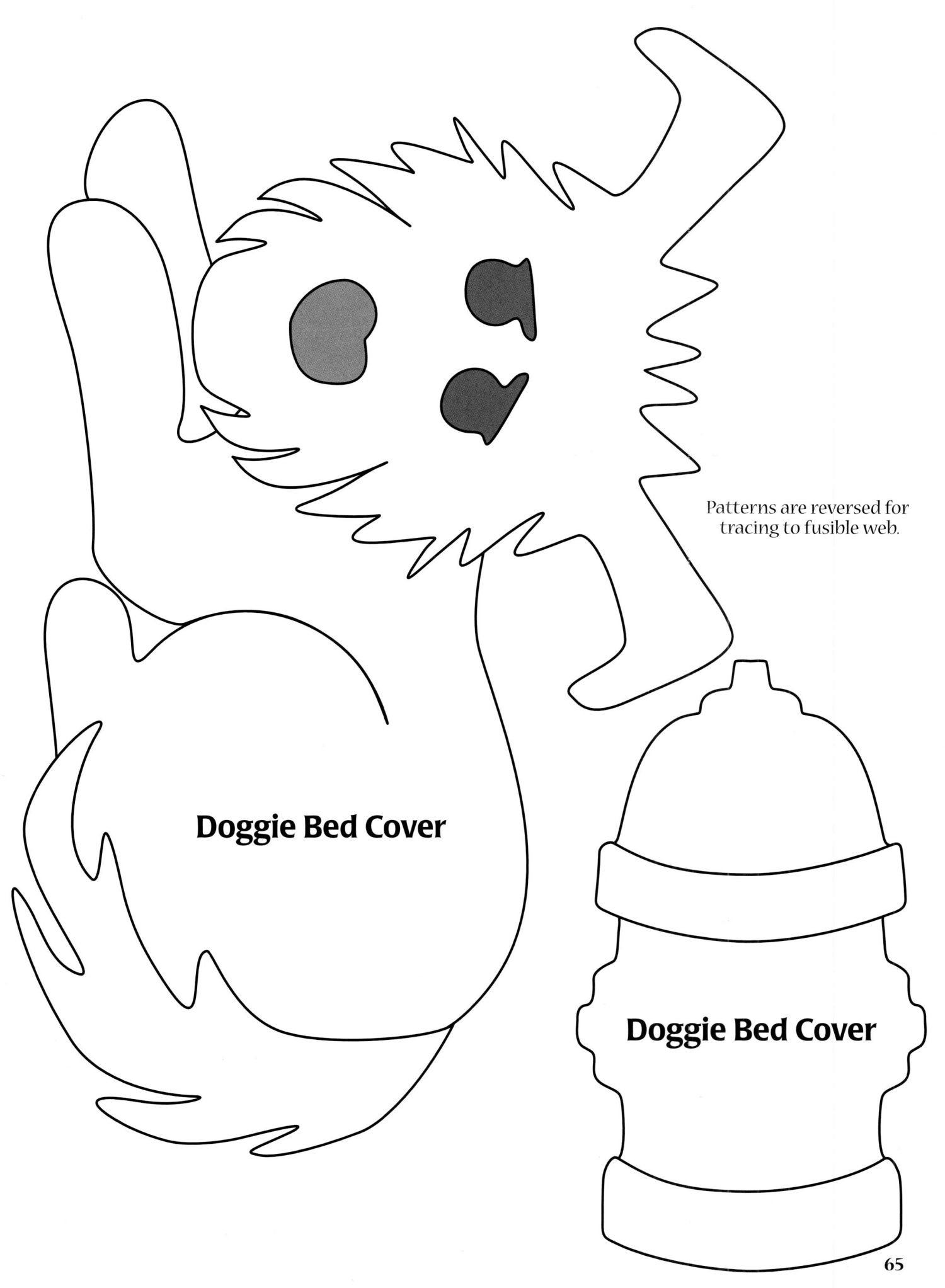

Patterns are reversed for tracing to fusible web.

Doggie Bed Cover

Doggie Bed Cover

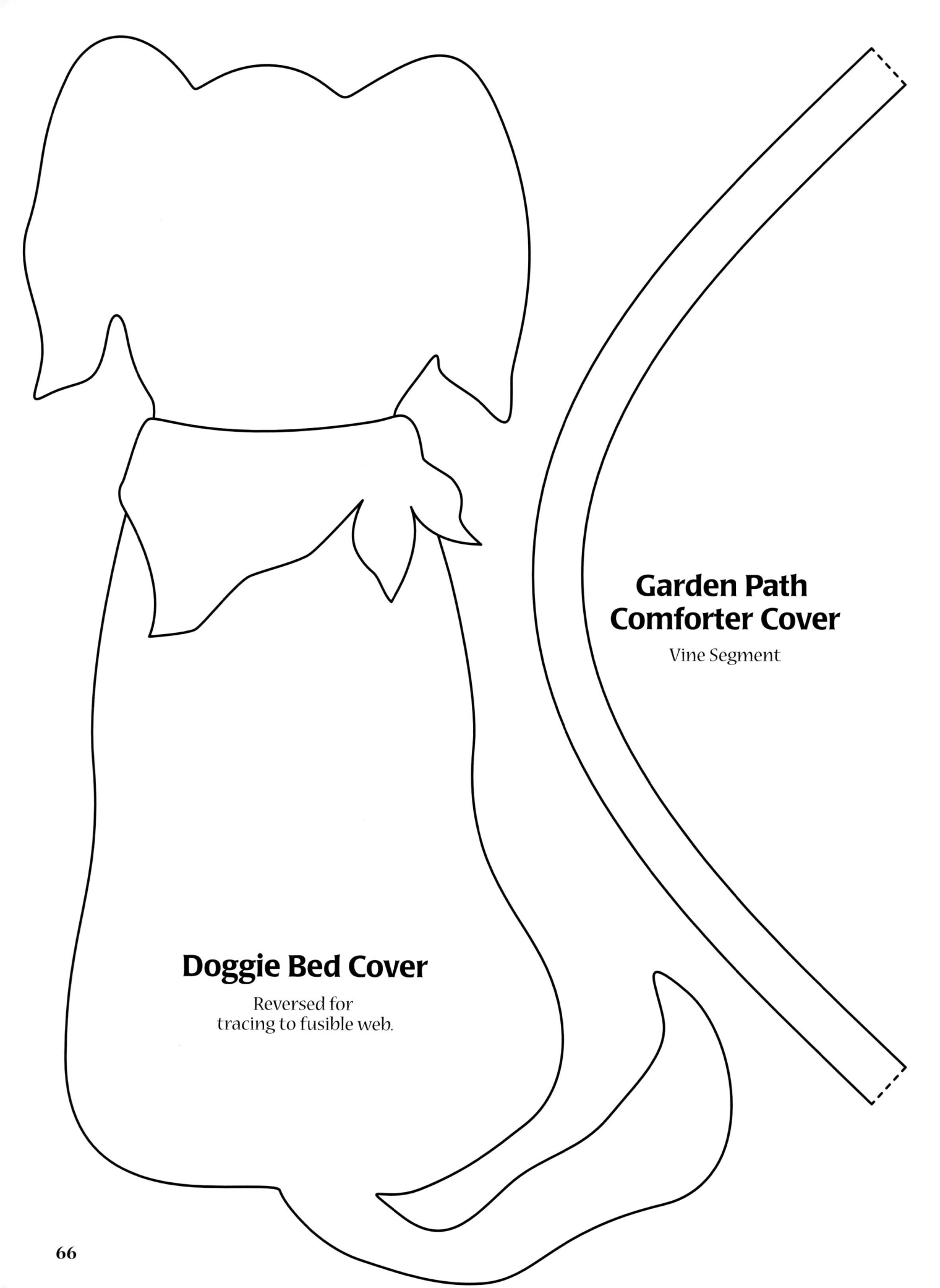

**Garden Path
Comforter Cover**

Vine Segment

Doggie Bed Cover

Reversed for
tracing to fusible web.

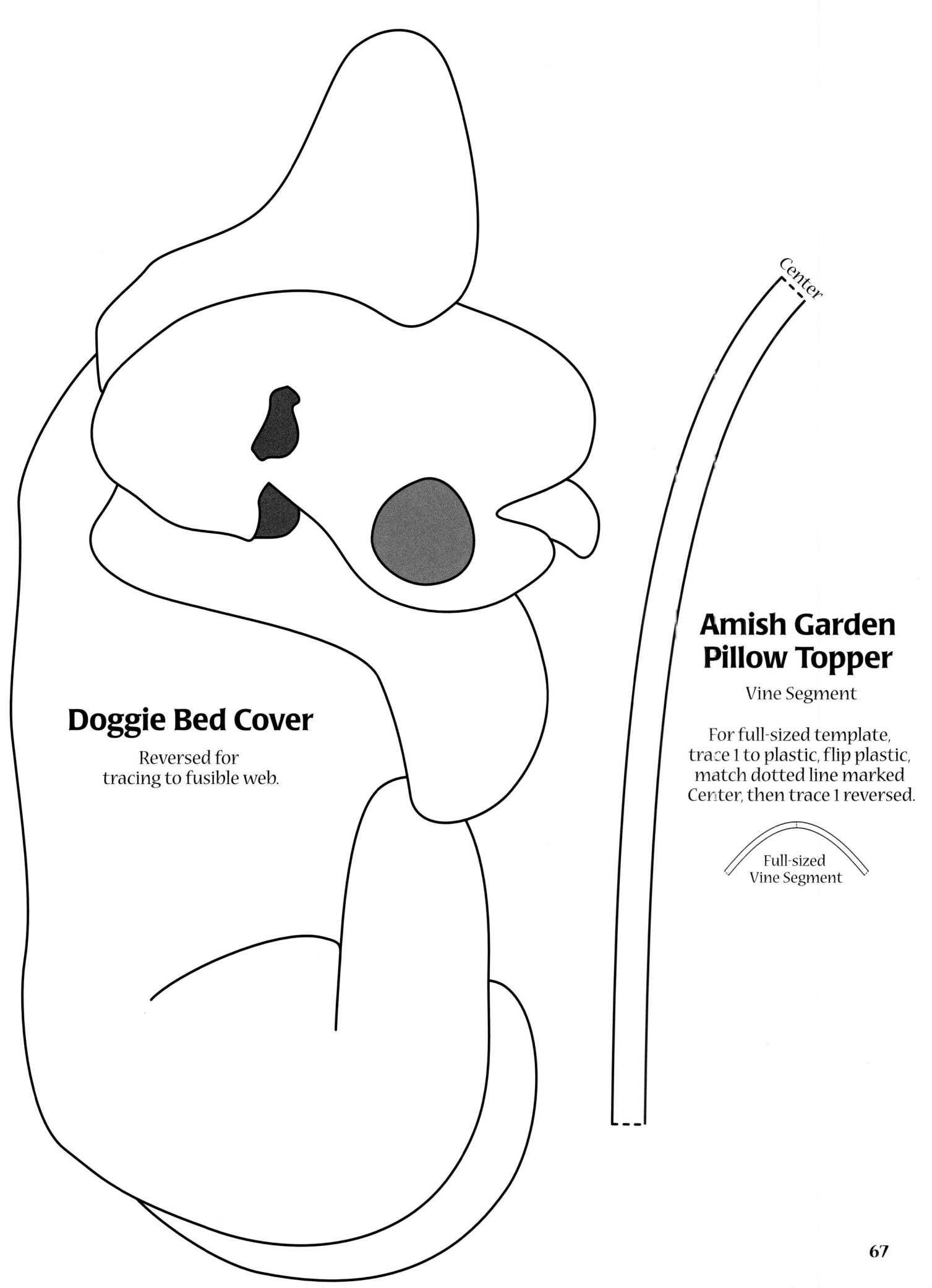

Doggie Bed Cover

Reversed for
tracing to fusible web.

Amish Garden
Pillow Topper

Vine Segment

For full-sized template,
trace 1 to plastic, flip plastic,
match dotted line marked
Center, then trace 1 reversed.

Center

Full-sized
Vine Segment

67

Doggie Bed Cover

Patterns are reversed for
tracing to fusible web.

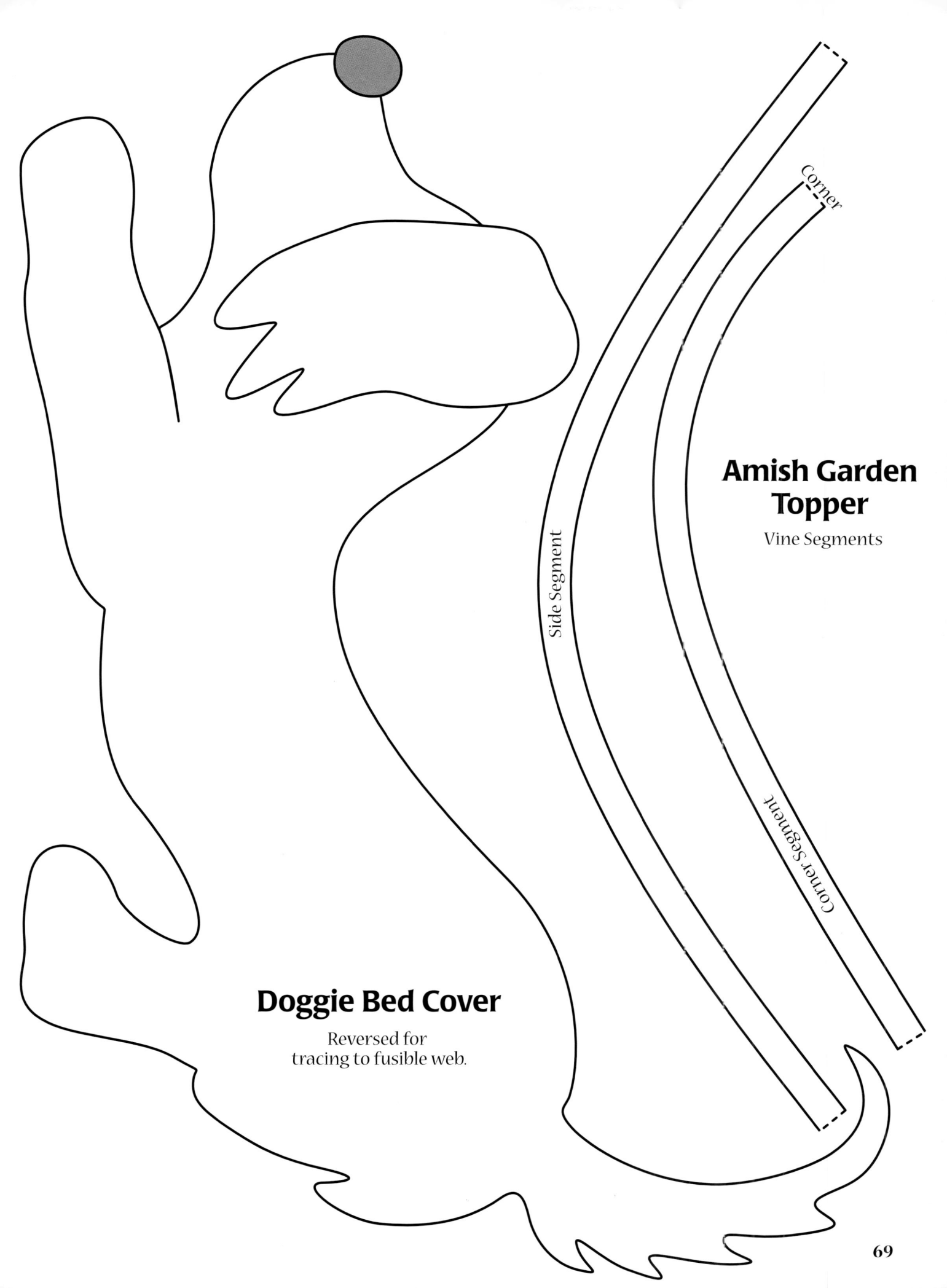

Amish Garden Topper

Vine Segments

Side Segment

Corner

Corner Segment

Doggie Bed Cover

Reversed for
tracing to fusible web.

69

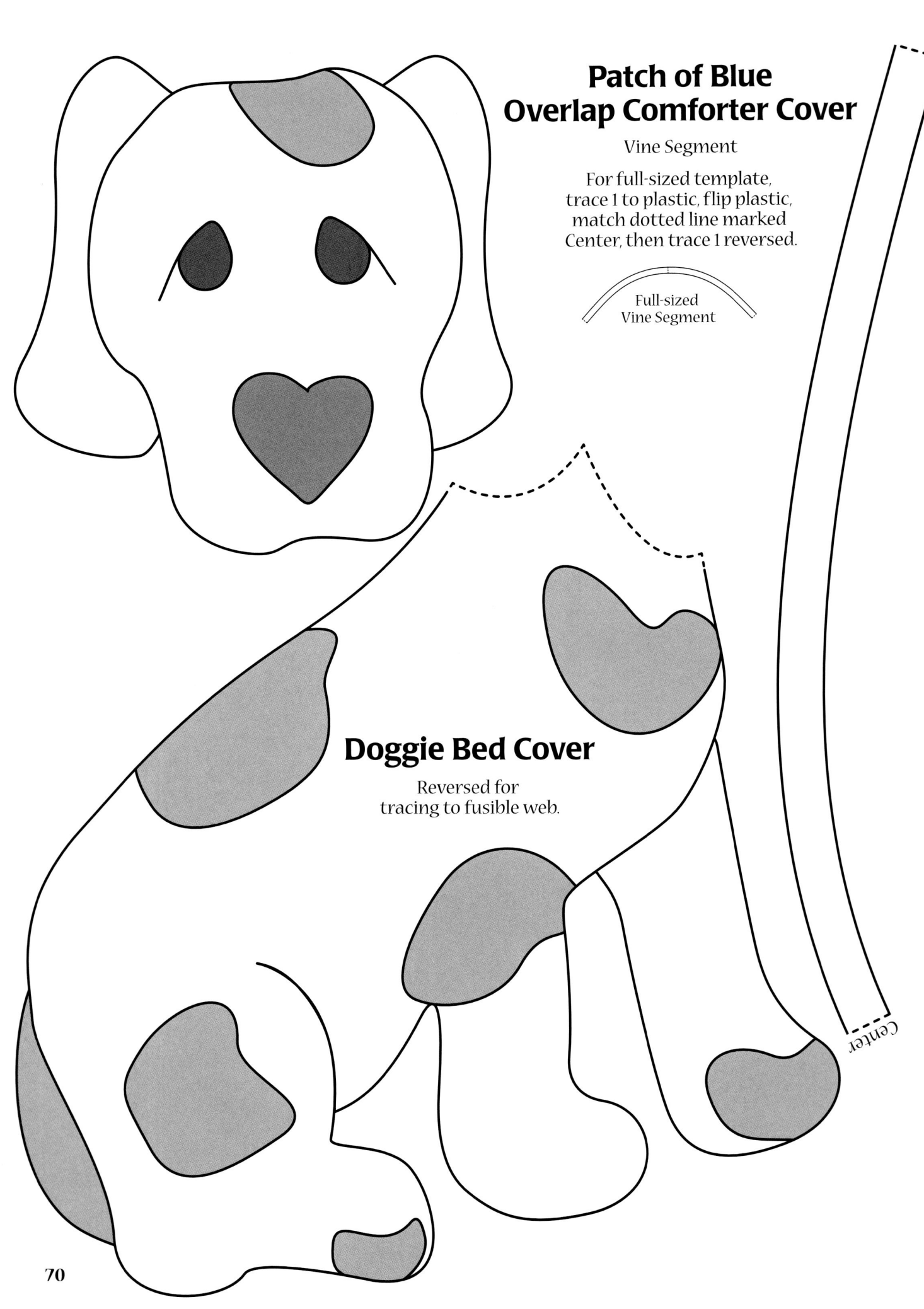

Patch of Blue
Overlap Comforter Cover

Vine Segment

For full-sized template,
trace 1 to plastic, flip plastic,
match dotted line marked
Center, then trace 1 reversed.

Full-sized
Vine Segment

Doggie Bed Cover

Reversed for
tracing to fusible web.

Center

Doggie Place Mat

Patterns are reversed for
tracing to fusible web.

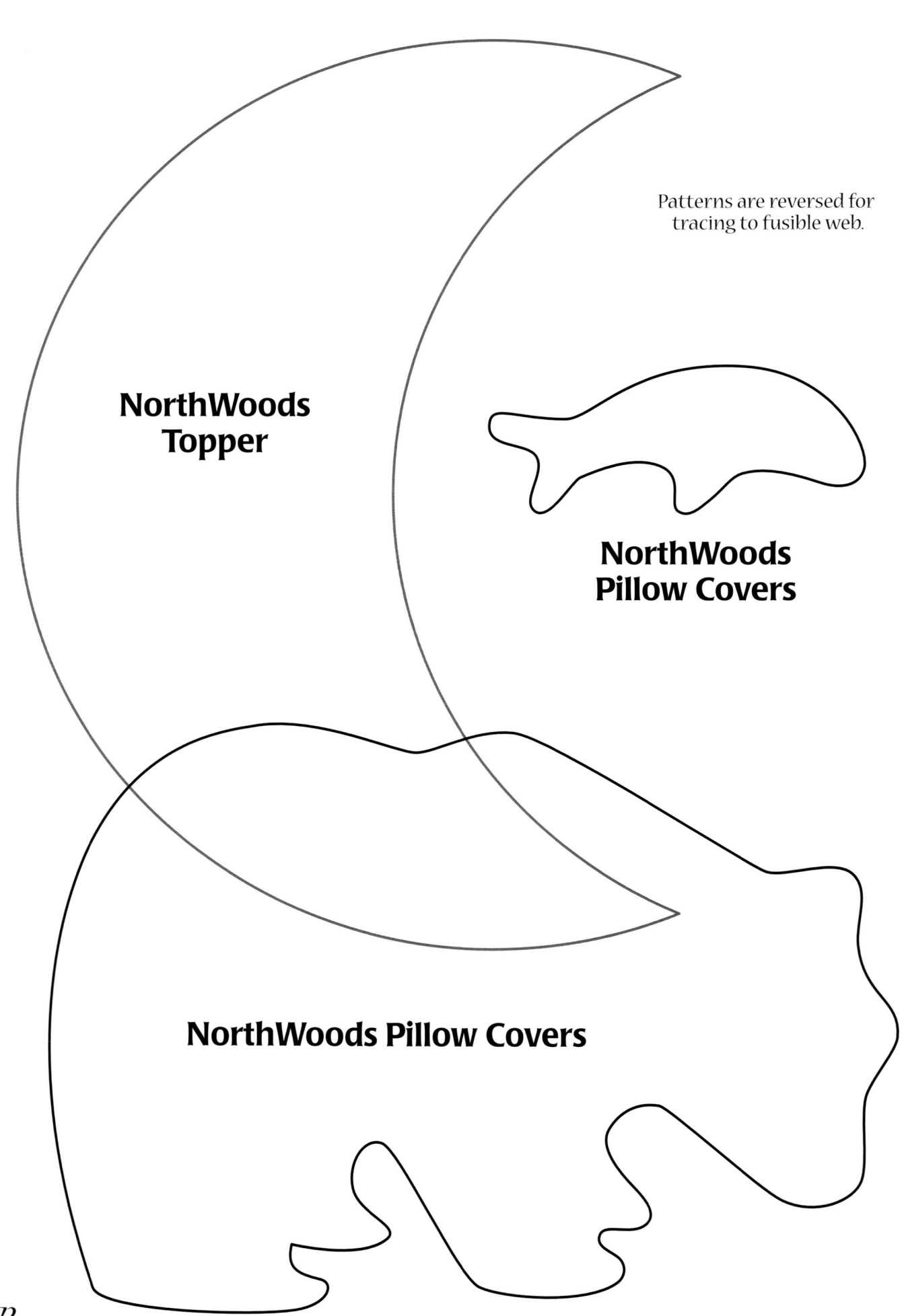

**NorthWoods
Topper**

Patterns are reversed for
tracing to fusible web.

**NorthWoods
Pillow Covers**

NorthWoods Pillow Covers

NorthWoods Topper

Make 200% photocopy for full-sized pattern.

NOTE: Copy page to 11x17" sheets of paper, if possible, and tape them together. Otherwise, tape 8½x11" copies together.

Permission granted to photocopy for individual use.

Patterns are reversed for tracing to fusible web.

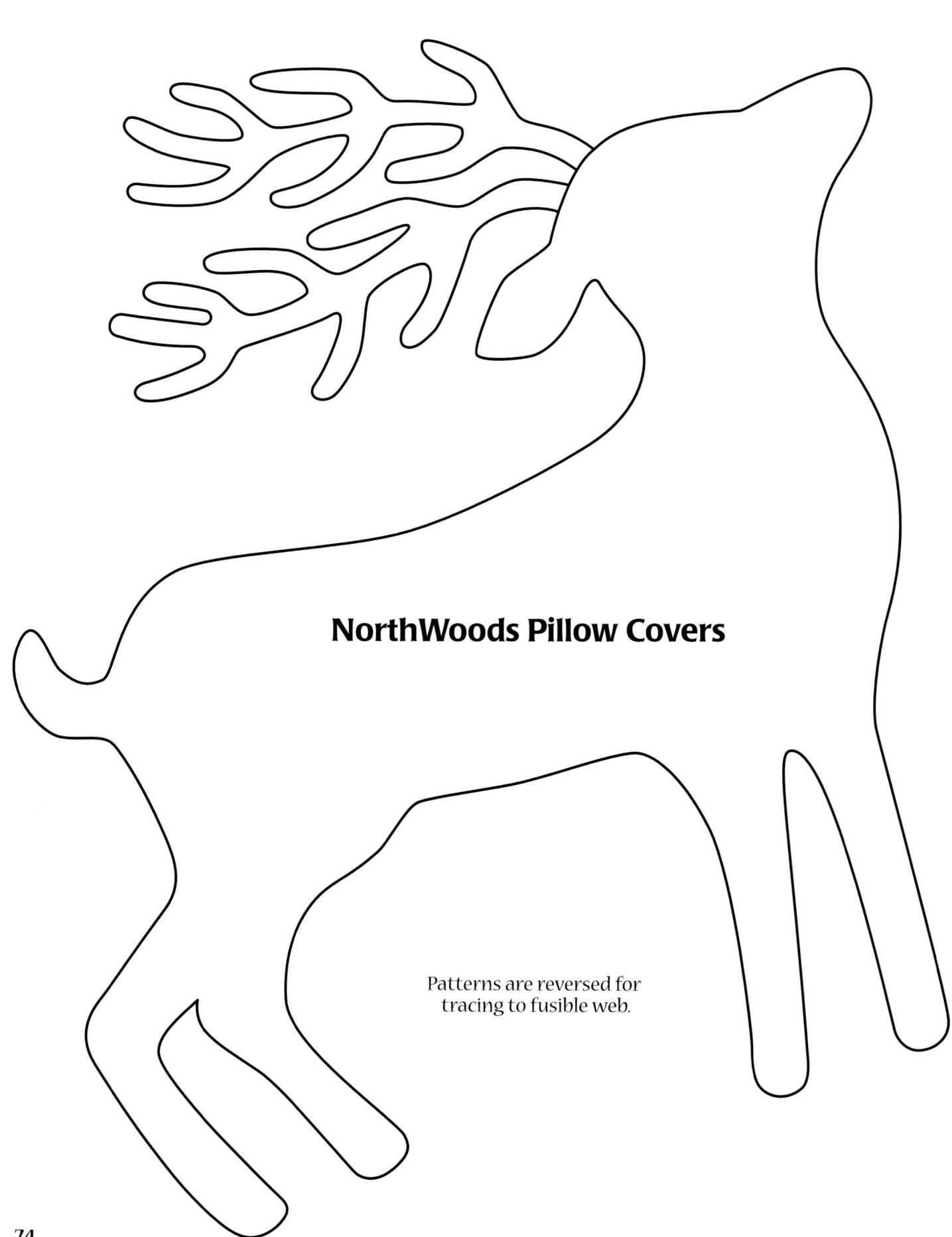

NorthWoods Pillow Covers

Patterns are reversed for
tracing to fusible web.

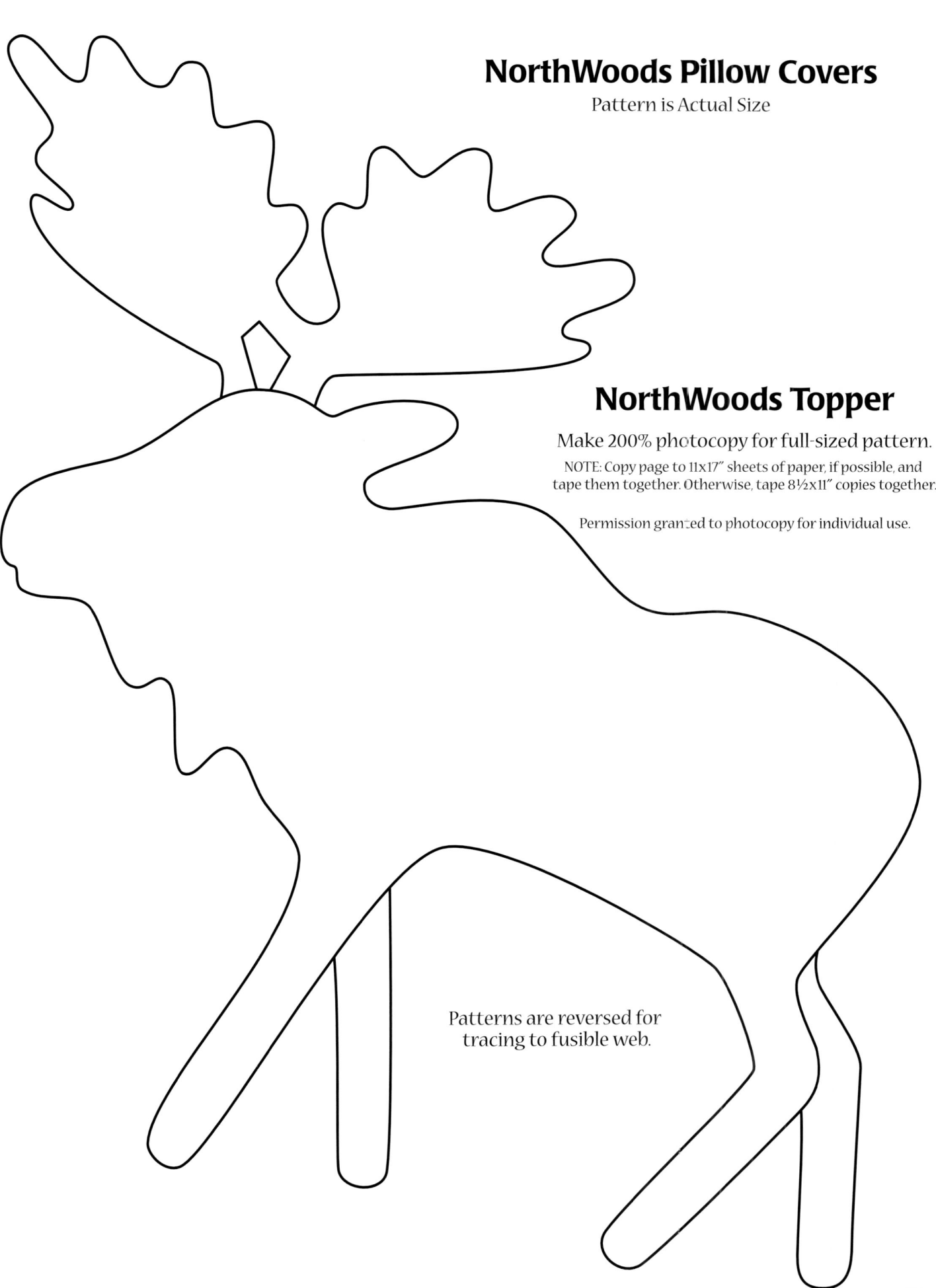

NorthWoods Pillow Covers
Pattern is Actual Size

NorthWoods Topper

Make 200% photocopy for full-sized pattern.

NOTE: Copy page to 11x17" sheets of paper, if possible, and tape them together. Otherwise, tape 8½x11" copies together.

Permission granted to photocopy for individual use.

Patterns are reversed for tracing to fusible web.

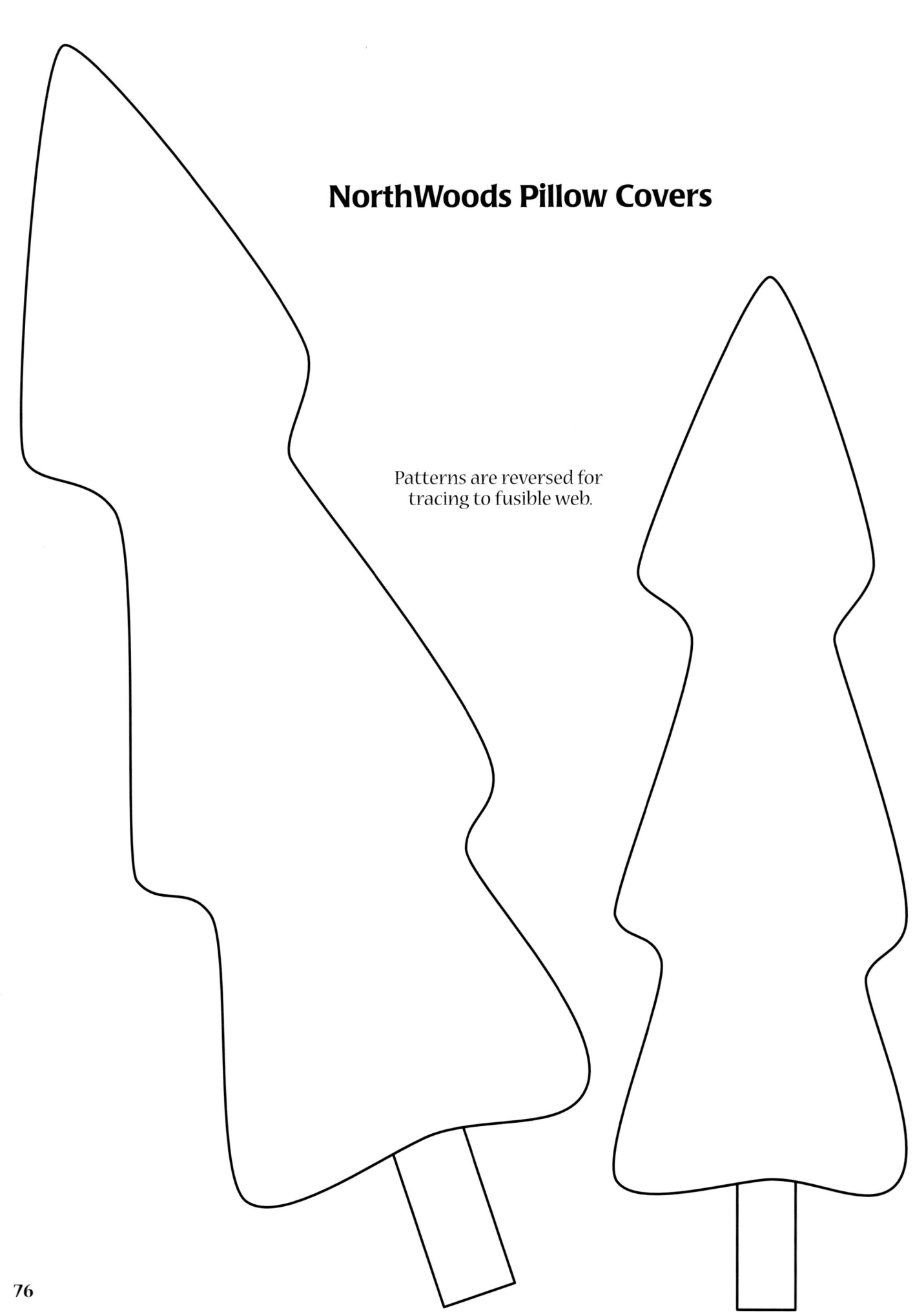

NorthWoods Pillow Covers

Patterns are reversed for
tracing to fusible web.

NorthWoods Pillow Covers

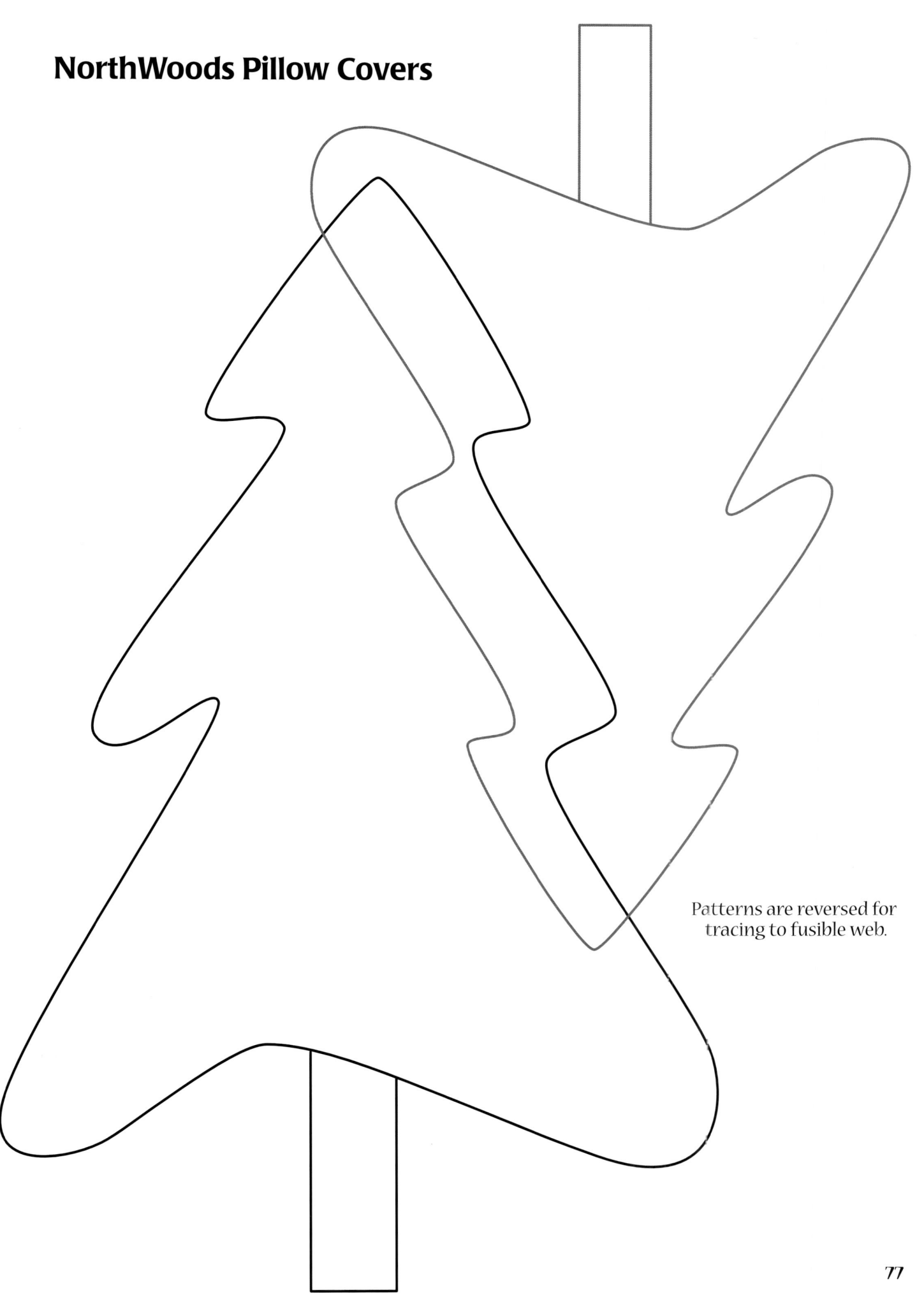

Patterns are reversed for tracing to fusible web.

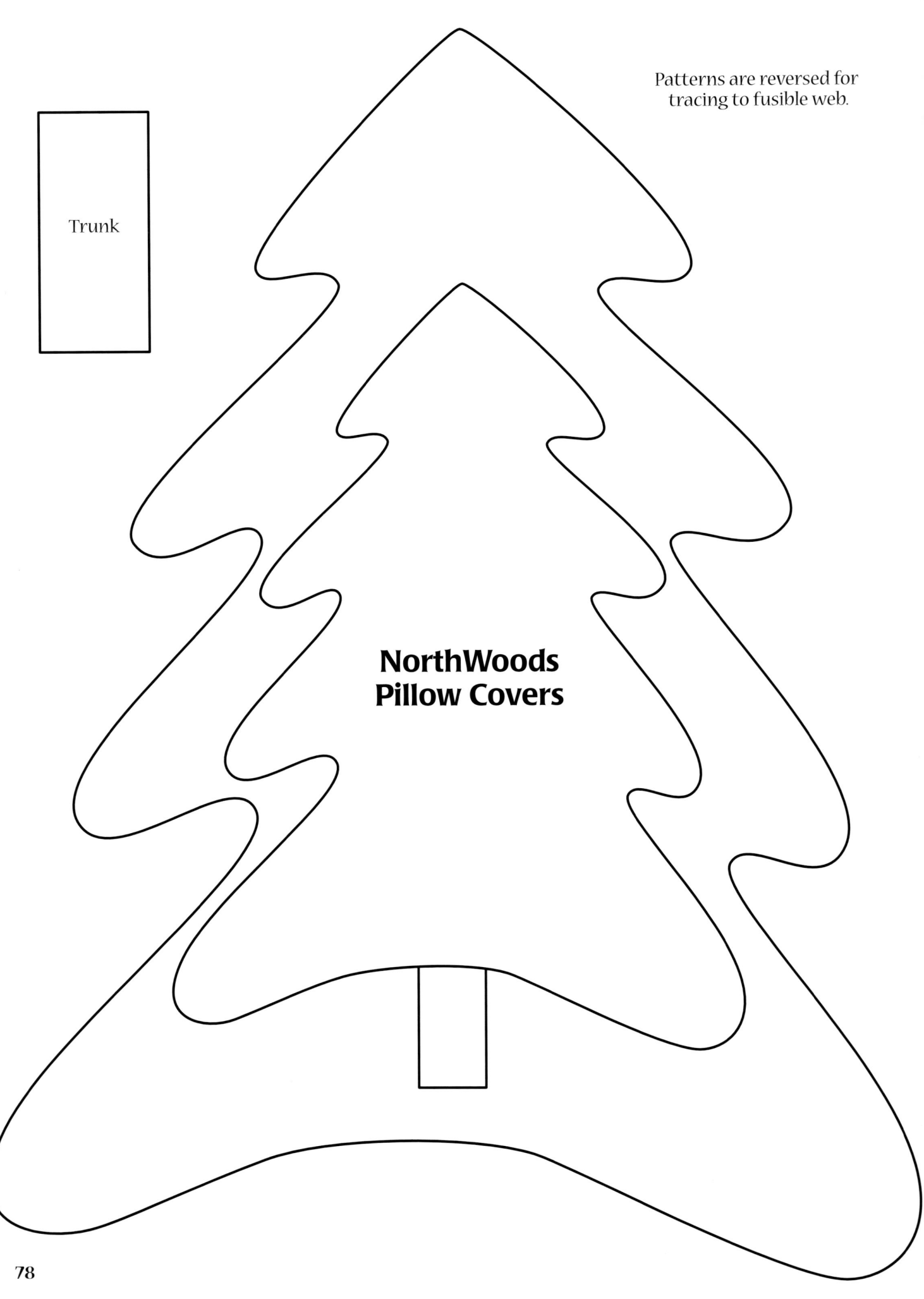

Trunk

Patterns are reversed for tracing to fusible web.

NorthWoods Pillow Covers

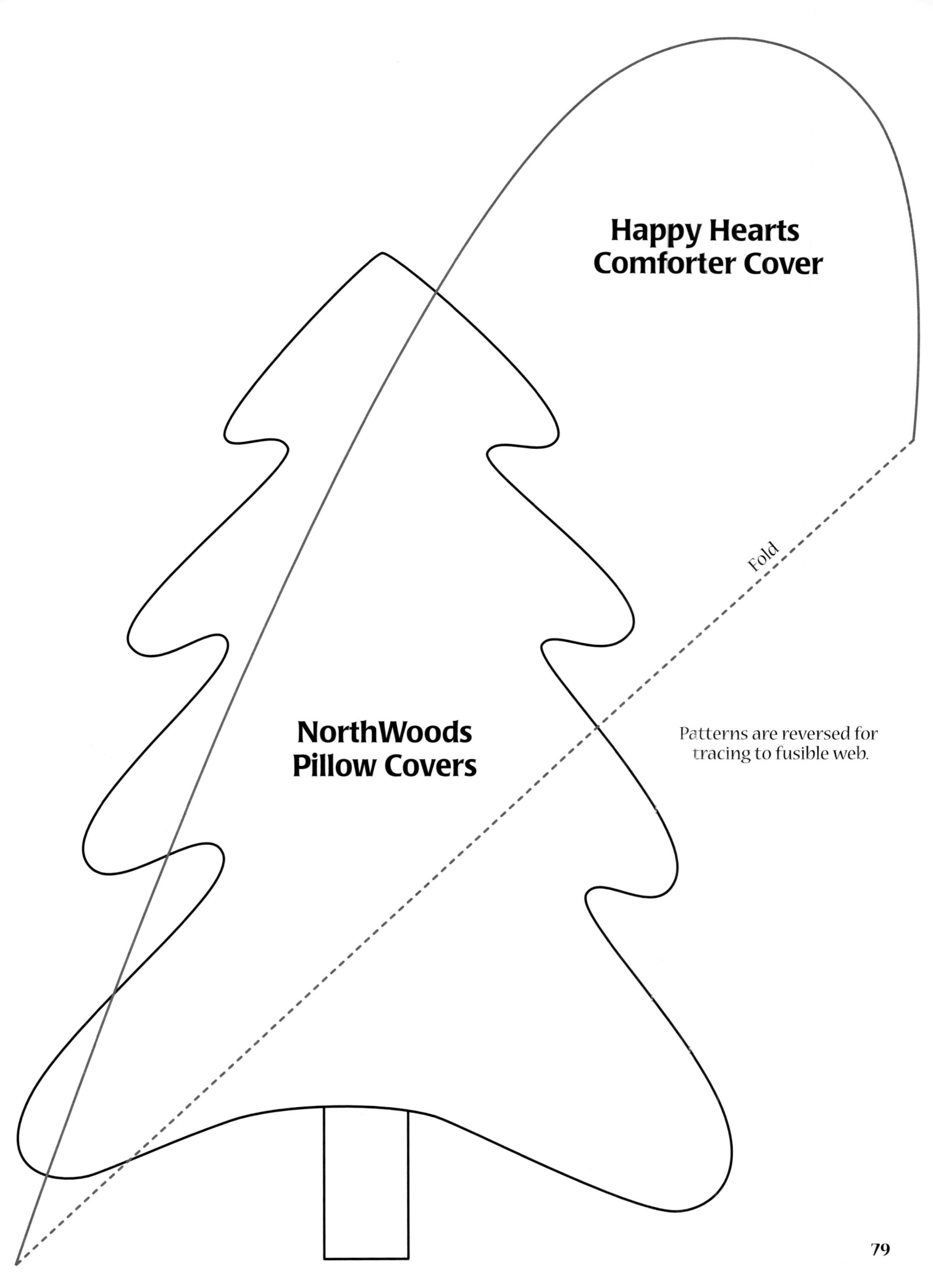

**Happy Hearts
Comforter Cover**

Fold

**NorthWoods
Pillow Covers**

Patterns are reversed for
tracing to fusible web.

Creative Fabric Ideas From Possibilities®

Cooking Possibilities

Quilters are super cooks as well! Over 100 recipes in this unique cookbook come from quilters across the country. Also included: quilting hints and quilted projects for the kitchen.

Joy to the World

Full of quilts for different skill levels, *Joy to the World* also contains delightful accessory projects such as stockings, tree skirts, gift bags, and place mats. Good recipes too!

Fashion Doll Fun

Introduce sewing to a new generation with *Fashion Doll Fun*. More than 20 patterns for dressing 11½" fashion dolls. Patterns are designed with a minimum number of seams.

5 Easy Pieces

Make use of the beautiful large florals now available to make custom decorator-style quilts and accessories. Large blocks and applique shapes help speed you along.

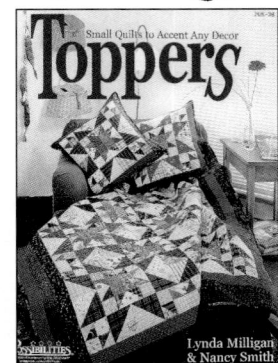

Toppers

Toppers are beautiful quilts for displaying over bed pillows, on a bedspread or comforter, or on the back of a couch. Since you are only making half a quilt, it only takes half the time!

HouseWarmers

Nineteen quilts and 25 project ideas for warming a home with the beauty of handmade quilts. Projects for every decor and skill level add personal touches to any room in the house.

Time for a Chain

This is the only Irish Chain book you will ever need! Detailed cutting charts give measurements for single, double, and triple Irish Chains in five sizes. Rotary cut for efficiency.

P.S. I Love You Two

A national top seller, this book includes quilts in three sizes–little, crib, & twin. Timeless projects make cherished gifts. Complete directions and a multitude of techniques.

P.S. I Love You

One of the top 10 quilting books in America. Includes 17 quilts in cradle, crib, and twin sizes. Also, nursery accessories for making darling children's rooms. Exceptional collection!

Pillow Patches

Making pillows has never been so easy or so much fun. Pillow covers can be changed at the flip of a button with the changing seasons. Over 25 designs take you through the year.

Album Coverups

Bring the creativity and fun of your memory book pages to the album cover. Use our ten great designs with easy fuse-and-use techniques to personalize your projects.

Possibilities®

…Publishers of DreamSpinners' patterns, I'll Teach Myself sewing products, and Possibilities' books…

Check with your local quilt shop. If not available, write or call us directly.

8970 East Hampden Avenue
Denver, Colorado 80231
303-740-6206 · Fax 303-220-7424
Orders only U.S. & Canada 1-800-474-2665
www.possibilitiesquilt.com

Quilts & More

This informative book has over 25 projects featuring photos transferred to fabric. Includes complete instructions and full-sized patterns for making family heirlooms.